BATH ENTERTAIN'D

Amusements, Recreations and Gambling
at the 18th-Century Spa

BATH ENTERTAIN'D

Amusements, Recreations and Gambling at the 18th-Century Spa

by Trevor Fawcett

RUTON : 1998

**To
Mary**

First published in the United Kingdom in 1998 by
RUTON, 25 Northampton Street, Bath, and produced by
R. Milsom & Associates 01454 850033

Copyright © Trevor Fawcett

ISBN 0-9526326-1-6

INTRODUCTION

Next to the medicinal waters and the comfortable Georgian lifestyle that Bath offered, its diversions were a prime attraction. 'Bath is certainly the very Theatre of variety in its amusements', ran one approving comment in 1779, and indeed, far from being peripheral to the spa's economic and social life, the fashionable entertainments were quite central to its continuing prosperity, its holiday atmosphere, and its alluring image. They were more varied than is commonly realised, appealing to humbler citizens as well the rich, and ranging from highly stuctured entertainments to casual pastimes and hobbies. Some had courtly origins (balls, cards, billiards, theatre), some were traditional (cockfights, racing, popular sports, civic ceremonies), but others belonged to the modern urban culture of coffee-houses, circulating libraries, exhibitions, public lectures and pleasure gardens. Healthy and relaxing open-air pursuits contrasted with the indoor excitements of assemblies and the gaming tables, but in one way or another, either as spectator or active participant, almost everyone was drawn into their orbit.

It took time for the full spread of amusements to develop. At first balls, concerts, plays and puppet shows were organised on a casual basis and even the gambling depended on who was in town. But by the 1720s an increasing flow of visitors (and the development of an autumn season) made investment in the leisure sector more worthwhile. At the same time risks were somewhat reduced through ticket subscription - a device which at least guaranteed promoters a financial return. As the attractions multiplied, the non-medical reasons for a trip to Bath became ever more persuasive. How much the amusements really amused depended on the company one was in at the time, and certainly they could stale with repetition. The 4th Earl of Chesterfield used to enjoy Bath, but eventually a sense of boredom overcame him whenever his health forced him back for yet another six weeks' cure. 'I am most excessively weary of this place, where the doing of nothings all day hinders one from doing anything', he wrote in December 1737. But dolce far niente *was of course much to the point. As Horace Walpole observed around the same date, Bath was 'a very proper place to do nothing in'. The easiest solution was to follow John Wood's advice and allow the amusements - 'Amusements so Sweet and Alluring' - to take over. The poet Alexander Pope in 1714 did just that - 'I have Slid, I cant tell how, into all the Amusements of this Place: My whole Day is shar'd by the Pump-Assemblies, the Walkes, the Chocolate houses, Raffling Shops, Plays, Medleys, &c.'. This kind of busy round, measured out by a timetable of socialising, became a central, repetitive theme of spa life. Not to join in was frowned on. If invalids were excused the stuffy Assembly Rooms, they were not absolved from all participation. The Penrose family, up from Cornwall in 1766 and expecting a quiet rest, found quite the reverse - 'Dinner time excepted... , we have no Respite. All is Hurry Hurry'. The effect could be less stimulating than stultifying, and some critics denounced the spa for its banal pleasures and essential frivolity. ' Here', wrote one in 1795, 'people must not be suffered to grow too serious. Bath is not a place to think in.'*

That, however, was to reduce the amusements to balls and card-parties, to fashion and trivia. The spectrum spread much further, as this volume goes to show. Not every recreation is covered here. Some were too informal or personal in character to be readily summarised. Much leisure time was after all spent in simply sightseeing about town, paying and re-paying social calls, holding tea-parties, dealing with tailors and dressmakers, reading and letter-writing, receiving music and drawing lessons, hobnobbing in taverns, scandalmongering, pursuing sex, fortune-hunting - or simply observing the passing scene, as one of Smollett's characters in Humphry Clinker *did, with amused pleasure at the 'general mixture of all degrees' to be seen in Bath's public places. Yet even without these, what the caricaturist Rowlandson called the 'Comforts of Bath', i.e. the more organised or public pastimes, are worth serious attention on the premise that the recreations of our ancestors amounted to more than a historical sideshow, that - like rock music or football today - they have a lot to tell about the society they belong to. This publication stops short of social analysis though. Its aim is rather to provide detailed and reliable information in easily accessible format. Packed with fresh detail, it can be read straight through for its own intrinsic interest, casually dipped into, or used for quick reference and as a springboard for further enquiry. For ease of consultation a dictionary style of presentation has been adopted, i.e. an alphabetical sequence of entries with appropriate cross-references to related topics.*

N.B. Certain entries quote sums of money. To obtain very approximate modern equivalents, multiply eighteenth-century amounts by at least fifty times, though because relative values have changed this will sometimes under- and sometimes overstate the comparison.

Angling

To fish the Bath waters required permission since the Corporation held most of the immediate river rights above and below the weir, and rented these rights out. Several fishermen made a commercial living from the river, but recreational angling too had plenty of devotees, the most famous instance being Princess Amelia, the spa's most regular royal visitor, who liked to cast her line from the summerhouse overlooking the Avon in the corner of Harrison's Gardens. Angling was a democratic sport appealing to all classes. Its popularity in the 1790s may be gauged by the presence of specialist suppliers at Bath. J.Grant at 5 Bridge Street, who claimed to have the biggest angling shop in the region, made artificial flies and other fishing tackle, and sold permits to fish for trout and eels in Wellow Brook. At the same period another dealer in angling gear, G.Yarnall, held fishing rights at Bathampton. He too made flies to order, which suggests that fly- not coarse-fishing was then the thing.

Antiquities

A letter sent by one spa visitor, Sir John Percival, in 1711 includes a careful Latin transcription from a Roman soldier's tombstone discovered during some road repairs - just one instance of the widespread curiosity that Bath's ancient relics aroused. Some were easily visible. Fragmentary inscriptions and carved faces and figures could be found embedded in the city walls and in buildings like the Abbey Church, where they made handy targets for boys throwing stones (as the antiquary William Stukeley noticed in 1723). John Wood's fantasy of Bath as a Druid capital (privately called 'a silly pack of stuff' by one opponent) stirred up further interest, and virtually anyone with a Classical education must have been thrilled by accidental Roman finds. In 1727 the gilt bronze head of Sulis Minerva turned up during work in lower Stall Street, a prized object soon to be reproduced in engraving and put on permanent display at the old Guildhall with a selection of Roman coins. Other discoveries followed, but none caused more excitement than the section of Roman *thermae* and several Saxon graves revealed in digging the foundations of the Kingston Baths in 1755. Among the sightseers were the Bath artist William Hoare and the Rev. Alexander Catcott of Bristol who both drew the site with details of the baths, hypocaust, pipes and mosaic.

Not until 1790 was there another find of such magnitude, when the rebuilding of the Pump Room brought to light stones and carvings from the ancient temple precinct. Again there was much fascinated interest. The politician Edmund Burke found it greatly entertaining to watch pieces of sculpture and Corinthian orders emerging from the earth almost daily. In 1792 another visitor, Louisa Holroyd, went to see the chief assembled fragments - 'a great many stones very well carved, a Medusa's Head in excellent preservation, a Jupiter and Juno, Diana's Head with her Crescent, parts of pillars etc. etc; skulls of Greyhounds, heifers, etc. that were sacrificed to the Deities...'. Antiquities found at Bath had sometimes been casually dispersed in the past. Even the elder John Wood had given valuable old coins away, and it remained easy enough for later antiquaries to make private collections. After 1790, however, the need for some sort of public archaeological museum became pressing, and in 1797 the Corporation at last approved plans to convert a house near the Cross and Hot baths for the purpose. With its exterior decorated by statues of King Edgar and old King Cole (from the former Guildhall façade), the new museum of 'mutilated altars and mouldering ornaments' was said in 1800 to be well frequented by cognoscenti.

Archery

Was it not surprising, queried an anonymous correspondent to the *Bath Herald* in summer 1792, that when other towns had brought back the manly sport of archery, Bath was still dragging its heels - 'and surely such healthful, bracing amusements' would be more beneficial than 'the very idle, enervating modes in which most of our Citizens dissipate their summer months'? Whether in response to this or not, it was soon possible to buy elegant bows and other equipment from Viner's perfume- and toyshop in [Old] Bond Street, and to try them out on targets set up in Grosvenor Gardens. This must have been a hobby more pursued by affluent residents than visitors.

Artists' Exhibitions and Studios

When Rowlandson caricatured the 'Comforts of Bath' around 1798, he pointedly included the society painter's studio among his objects of satire. This is how we tend to imagine spa portraiture, in terms of the wealthy sitter, the fashionable artist, and the oil canvas, whereas the bulk of the output, especially later in the century, was in miniatures, profiles and silhouettes, not so much pictorial expressions of wealth and status as modest 'likenesses' for family and friends. Even so, whatever the scale or the expense, having one's 'face taken' meant visiting the chosen artist's rooms - a small adventure for some, a boring procedure for others, yet always with a hint of vanity on the sitter's part, some consideration of what to wear and what attitude to strike. The actual sitting might be brief, even mechanical in the case of profilists who relied on optical devices, or it might require return visits over several days, but for the most part it was a strictly businesslike occasion (the young Thomas Lawrence being unusual in tolerating the sitter's relations and acquaintance in his painting room).

The chief pleasure in visits to artists' studios lay rather in sampling their exhibitions, often arranged in a separate room which a servant would show to any genteel caller. Displays of work were valuable self-advertisements and might bring in a useful income from entrance charges - enough to pay the rent, Wright of Derby discovered, when he was at Bath in 1776. From the visitor's point of view a private exhibition was a pleasant morning 'lounge', a talking point later, and a chance to size up different artists' styles and skills in advance of commissioning a portrait or choosing a drawing master. Oil painters such as William Hoare, Thomas Gainsborough, Thomas Beach, and R.E.Pine, all had quite smart addresses and elegant well-lit showrooms. Mrs Delany called to see Gainsborough's pictures in 1760 and found them 'splendid impositions', and we have reports of other visitors in the 1770s viewing Hoare's and Gainsborough's exhibitions in quick succession. After 1780, as the population of resident and visiting artists expanded, one-man shows were advertised more often. The Viennese profilist Charles Rosenberg had copies of the many celebrities who had sat to him on constant display at his rooms on North Parade. Similarly Joseph Hutchisson showed nearly 200 portraits in 1798, and the younger Thomas Robins arranged viewings of his paintings of exotic flora and fauna, and Ferdinand Becker of highly finished landscape watercolours, to give but a few examples. In 1793 over a hundred youthful works of the local prodigy Thomas Barker hung at Spackman's exhibition gallery in Monmouth Street. Other artists exhibited at Rickards' printshop or, still more publicly, at the Pump Room - until the Corporation forbade the practice because nailing up pictures was defacing the walls. The mixed artists' exhibition held at Thomas Beach's house in Westgate Buildings in 1778, one of the earliest of its kind outside London, was a more fitting and co-operative publicity device.

Virtuosi of art could be indulged in ways other than artists' exhibitions. Private collectors might open their doors to suitable callers. Auction rooms were more easily accessible and sometimes resembled little picture galleries in the days leading up to sales. Saleable old masters hung in other dealers' rooms as well, for example at the still-life painter William Jones's house in Gallaway's Buildings from 1769 to 1774 and at Spackman's gallery in the 1790s. Not far away at Corsham the impressive Methuen collection awaited inspection (68 items worth £30,000, reported one viewer from Bath in 1780). It was possible too at different times to enjoy huge panoramas of sea battles painted on canvas, scandalous political images in printshop windows, and exhibitions of pictures done in needlework, 'polygraphic' reproductions, religious sculpture, ivories, and collections of plaster casts. Nor should the decorative arts be overlooked, whether the fine porcelain, silverware, pattern fabrics and other goods on show at specialist retailers, or the craftsmanship of Bath statuaries and stonemasons to be seen at their workshops. Visits to the latter might lead to commissions not just in Bath but through much of the West Country.

••• See also **Auctions; Exhibitions.**

Assemblies and Assembly Rooms

Any prearranged gathering of polite company might be termed an assembly, but here the word is restricted to public socialising at the various Assembly Rooms (occasionally the Guildhall) under the authority of a master-of-ceremonies. Assemblies in this sense originated before 1700 with the small-scale balls for the visiting élite, sometimes presided over by the Duke of Beaufort, held in the upstairs room of the old Guildhall. Gradually it became apparent that a more suitable venue was needed, not merely for balls but for the insatiable gambling which seasonally gripped Bath. The royal court's sojourns at the spa in 1702 and 1703 underlined yet again the need for investment in better facilities, but not until 1709 did a London entrepreneur, Thomas Harrison, risk building the first simple two-storey Assembly Room near Gravel Walks, abutting the outside of the city walls and with enclosed gardens (reached by 'Hanging-Stairs') running down to the river. The Corporation objected to the venture as an interference in city interests, but the visiting company approved. It was an institution geared to their needs - meeting place, casino, café, and ballroom rolled into one - financed by the rake-off from gambling, the sale of refreshments (as well as snuff, gloves, cards and dice), plus the guinea subscription for access to Harrison's Walks. Only much later did it become transparent how strong a financial stake

Beau Nash, the indispensable master-of-ceremonies, had in its success. A satirical pamphlet of the period cast him as 'Rover' to Harrison's 'Thrifty', and portrayed them as equals in the plot to milk the visitors, Nash's role being to lure rich clients to Bath and then to the Assembly Room. Gambling therefore had the highest priority. 'Play' - meaning cards and dice (and sooner or later billiards) - was the chief business, with balls, musical 'medleys' and other entertainments secondary and more dependent on private sponsorship. In general the round of diversions required Nash's presence and the season sprang to life only with his reappearance in Bath from London or Tunbridge Wells. In his absence, or if Harrison's were closed, the company resorted to other gambling rooms like Dame Lindsey's (installed by 1721, it seems, in an imposing new house built against the Abbey Church in Gravel Walks). Until 1730, however, Harrison's alone offered the complete facilities, further improved by a purpose-built ballroom added in 1720. Having a monopoly, however, he overexploited it, and in the end it was public complaint about his high charges that led Nash to back Humphrey Thayer's project for alternative Assembly Rooms.

Thayer, an opulent London druggist who already leased the nearby bowling green and shops on Terrace Walk, therefore included a complete suite of Rooms in John Wood's redevelopment scheme for the area, though lingering doubts about their viability can be seen in his wish for a flexible design that would allow the building to be adapted if necessary to other uses. Launched with a breakfasting and a ball in April 1730, and initially under the management of the former opera-singer (and proven hostess) Dame Lindsey, in the event it complemented rather than competed with Harrison's - even to the extent of a brief connivance in price-fixing between them when Lindsey's sister, Elizabeth Hayes, succeeded Harrison in 1731/2. The older establishment still had advantages in its adjacent garden and in the downstairs playhouse opened in 1732, but otherwise Nash treated both places even-handedly, sharing out the card assemblies and balls on different days through the week to save unnecessary competition. Both venues soon acquired fresh names. Hayes' became Hawley's through her marriage to Francis, 2nd Lord Hawley, and Dame Lindsey's decease in 1737 brought her capable ex-housekeeper Catherine Lovelace onto the scene. To Lovelace's, which had the larger ballroom at this date, fell the honour of holding the grand ball and supper for the Prince of Wales in 1738.

Such special events aside, assemblies were now organised in subscription series, one in autumn, the other in spring, alternating between the two Rooms. Subscription money mainly went towards music for both the balls and the Pump Room, the same band performing at each. The Rooms were rewarded by the profits from selling refreshments during the interval, and Nash provided his own services free. The duty of any master-of-ceremonies was most onerous during the French dances, since in all the panoply of Bath's diversions it was this first stage of a full dress assembly that allowed rank and privilege their fullest expression. He must therefore ensure that titled women secured the best seats, that every nicety of formal dress was observed, and that individual couples were led out to dance in exact order of precedence. Nash indeed orchestrated the whole show. If male minuet dancers were scarce, he took their place. He made introductions, regulated the music, and decreed when the tea break should come or the English country dances take over - at which point decisions on precedence (who should start at the top of the line) might be left to the dancers themselves. While dancing was in progress, another room held the inveterate card-players over whom Nash also exerted nominal control. The entire assembly operated in fact within a fixed and ordered framework down to that precise moment at which Nash's watch (itself set by the Pump Room's Tompion clock) registered eleven and the dancing and the cards ceased.

So lengthy was Nash's reign and such was his standing that his death in 1761 put the assemblies in some danger, for they were difficult organisms to manage and neither of his immediate successors, his former deputy Collett and the often ridiculed Derrick, had his presence, connections, or sources of outside income. Eventually the factions into which the company was divided erupted into violent confrontation in 1769 over the candidate to succeed Derrick. The compromise choice of William Wade failed to prevent further dissent in 1774 about the limits of his authority, which was now inextricably linked with the rivalries of the Assembly Rooms. These institutions had been evolving since the days of Hawley and Lovelace. Both had been affected by the bans on various games of chance, which drove heavy gambling away but filled the void with regular card assemblies in milder forms. The Simpsons, first father then son, became tenants of Hawley's and in 1749-50 undertook a major extension. A spacious ballroom (90' in length) with high stuccoed ceiling was built over a new basement theatre, allowing the two earlier ballrooms to be turned into coffee-room (40') and cardroom

(60'). In elegance and capacity, to say nothing of the rural views from its windows, Simpson's now had a decided edge over its competitor, Wiltshire's, which until then had boasted the superior ballroom (86'). For the next six years Simpson's theatre also pitted itself against the rival Orchard Street establishment until Simpson finally obtained the compensation he demanded to close it down.

For twenty years Simpson's and Wiltshire's (the latter known as Gyde's from 1767) shared the balls, card assemblies, concerts, occasional lectures and exhibitions on a fairly equitable basis, keeping the focus of the amusements in the lower town. By the mid-1760s, though, the Lansdown suburbs were again expanding and in November 1764 the younger John Wood announced plans for a tavern (later changed to a theatre), coffee house, and complete set of Assembly Rooms to be raised just north-west of Queen Square and financed through a company of shareholders. This was the germ of the Upper Assembly Rooms, constructed instead on a site near the Circus and opened with a famous ridotto (to which leading Bath citizens were for once invited) in

*William Dawson
Master-of-Ceremonies
at the Upper Rooms
1777-85*

September 1771. Altogether more luxurious than the two older institutions, its arrival had an immediate impact on their fortunes. Faced with the competition, within weeks the former Gyde's Rooms ceased to function and Simpson retired. Gyde took his place and moved into the vacated premises across Terrace Walk - only to suffer a continued drain of custom to the glamour and novelty of the Upper Rooms. Within a few years the latter was building coffee and billiard rooms at the front and an extra card room at the rear, while Gyde could only dream about realising the wonderful extension (with a new ballroom and a 200' walk) the architect Palmer had designed for him.

From the start there was bad blood between the Upper Rooms and new Gyde's over the musicians and over support for the Pump Room. Worse still, the attempt by the Upper Rooms' management committee in 1774 to curtail the freedom of the master-of-ceremonies, William Wade, to run the assemblies as he thought fit had the joint subscribers to both Rooms in uproar, with heated partisanship and boycotts on both sides. Peace was restored, but when Wade departed in 1777 it was agreed to have separate M.C.s in future, Dawson thereby being elected to the Upper Rooms and Tyson to Gyde's. Personally they co-operated, and the master-of-ceremony's benefit balls (the gentlemanly device adopted after Nash's time to reimburse office-holders) saw high attendances of around 1000 at both Rooms. Yet the Upper Rooms' shareholders, overanxious to protect their investment, continued to upset the fragile balance and by 1783 the result was only too plain - 'the Old Rooms sink under the weight of personal influence'. This adverse competition was also damaging the whole lower town in its commercial tug-of-war with fashionable upper Bath, the more so as it seemed that Gyde's could no longer even pay its share towards the Pump Room concerts. But in autumn 1784 Gyde and Tyson put forward a new subscription package by which they guaranteed no fewer than 14 'dress' and 20 'cotillion' balls that season. This was the start of a twenty-year rally by the shabby but still comfortable and convenient Lower Rooms. A year later Gyde handed over to his nephews, the Heaven brothers. About the same time Tyson moved to the Upper Rooms and the immensely popular James King stepped into the place thus vacated at the Lower Rooms. Only the annoying counter-attraction of private routs prevented these from being boom years at the (now more co-operative) pair of Assembly Rooms, especially as cotillions and fancy balls were so much the rage and the rather tiresome ritual of minuets was in decline.

The Bath assemblies - so influential a model for gatherings of town and country gentry throughout the kingdom - were at their best polite, glittering, modish showcases for the propertied, the well-bred, and the beautifully clad (the ladies 'as fine as Sattins and feathers could make them', noted Elizabeth Sheridan in 1786). Still it required constant effort to keep them so. Almost all the M.C.s issued codes of dress and conduct, occasionally revised in line with current fashions but always insistent on protocol and decorum. Men wearing riding boots, women an apron or the wrong sort of hat or hoop, could easily come in for censure. More difficult was to maintain class barriers, as the numbers attending assemblies grew and the subscription system meant tickets being passed around. In later decades there were periodic complaints about the infiltration of people 'whose dress and station in life does not entitle them to associate with people of distinction' (1772); about 'Servants, Hair-dressers, and other improper persons' occupying seats intended for people of fashion' (1778); about actors and musicians intruding into card assemblies or walking about the Rooms (1795). On the other hand the learned professions were welcome to subscribe, and if a scrupulous parson like John Penrose stayed away, many clergy (and indeed Penrose's own daughter) found assemblies irresistible. The fact that people in trade were debarred had the effect of excluding the majority of Bath's Corporation. Their response from about 1779 was to establish assemblies, under their own master-of-ceremonies and in the stuccoed and chandeliered splendour of the new Guildhall, that were hardly less attractive than those of the Upper Rooms itself. The Mayor's entertainment for the Princes of Wales and Orange and 500 guests in January 1797 - formal ball, supper, glee-singing, then country dancing until 4 a.m. - showed just how far the bourgeoisie had progressed.

••• *Postscript 1. The two Lower Assembly Rooms (i.e. in the lower part of town) were always named after their current proprietors. So the original Rooms were successively called Harrison's (from Thomas Harrison) 1709-31/2; Hayes' or Hawley's (from Elizabeth Hayes, later Lady Hawley, sister of Dame Lindsey) 1731/2-45; Simpson's (from William Simpson until 1755, then his son Charles) 1745-71; Gyde's (from Cam Gyde) 1771-85; and Heaven's (from Thomas and then James Heaven, Gyde's nephews) 1785 onwards. The second Rooms, having been financed by Humphrey Thayer, were sometimes known as Thayer's, but otherwise went under the proprietors' names, viz. Lindsey's (from*

*Dame Lindsey) 1730-37; Lovelace's (from Catherine Lovelace) 1737-
44; Wiltshire's (from Ann Wiltshire until 1747, John Wiltshire until 1762,
then Walter) 1744-67; Gyde's (from Cam Gyde) 1767-71. In 1771, when
these Rooms closed, Gyde took over the original Rooms from Simpson
and, at the risk of confusing posterity, reapplied his name to these instead.
The Rooms built near the Circus were usually referred to as the New or
Upper Assembly Rooms until 1820 (when the remaining Lower Rooms
were gutted by fire) and after that time simply as the Assembly Rooms.
Under a committee of shareholders they were rented and managed by
different wine-merchants - Robert Hayward 1771-79; Ann Hayward
1779-82; Henry Derham 1782-86; Henry Derham & William Stroud
1786-96; William Stroud 1796 onwards.*

   ••• **Postscript 2.** *The master-of-ceremonies' sequence began with
Captain Webster c.1703-05, continued by Richard Nash 1705-61, James
Collett (Jacques Caulet) 1761-63, Samuel Derrick 1763-69, [William
Brereton 1769], and William Wade 1769-77. Once the office was split
in two, the sequence proceeded at the Upper Rooms with William Dawson
1777-85 and Richard Tyson 1785-1805, and at the Lower Rooms with
William Brereton 1777-80, Richard Tyson 1780-85 and James King 1785-
1805. M.C.s officiating at the City Assembly in the Guildhall were Simeon
Moreau, Hanbury Pettingal, Charles Mercie, and James Marshall.*

   ••• See also **Cards**; **Dancing**; **Gambling**; **Guildhall**; **Pump Room**;
Routs.

Auctions

In the eighteenth century auctions developed into big business. After
1750 advertisements of sales increasingly filled many columns of local
newspapers, and at Bath the names of Trimnell, Evatt, Cross, Birchall,
Plura, Evill, and other prominent auctioneers were forever in the public
eye. Most of them took up auctioneering via the upholstery trade, which
now embraced the whole of general house furnishing and interior
decoration, and from that the work of clearing houses and the re-sale of
goods and properties. Although auctions could be humdrum affairs, they
sometimes offered special interest and entertainment value. As late as
1795 William Evill organised an evening sale of linen drapery and
haberdashery at his Milsom Street rooms 'by the Candle', a reference
not to the illumination but to the old system of accepting the highest bid
before a short candle went out, a more dramatic method than normal
bidding - hence his promise to keep out improper persons and stop

impudent children from attending. Certain property sales might arouse a good deal of curiosity, but for moneyed visitors and residents alike the specialist auctions of chinaware, jewellery, wines, books, fossils, antiquities, and the like, and above all works of art, probably commanded most attention.

By the last quarter of the century Bath was becoming a major centre of art dealing. Two entries from Edmund Rack's journal in February 1780 highlight the trend: 'afternoon went to view a fine collection of Paintings just come from London for Sale by Auction' and 'Attended an Auction of Pictures in which were some Capital peices [*sic*] by Italian Masters'. More and more pictures were pouring on to the English market from abroad, and the French Revolution would soon unleash a further flood. Bath auctioneers benefited from all this, as well as from the dispersal of local collections like those of Dr Rice Charleton (1788), George James of Kelston (mainly choice Italian drawings, 1792) or the artist William Hoare (1794). High-sounding names in the catalogues cannot of course be taken just at face value. 'Undoubted works' of Leonardo, Raphael, Titian, Rubens, Rembrandt and others would mostly be copies, 'school of', or actual fakes, but many lesser attributions (out of the c.200 artists cited in the dozen years 1788-1800 alone) may well be correct, including most of the British names. The lists demonstrate anyway that Italian, Dutch and Flemish landscapes made up the largest category, followed by religious, genre, marine, and other paintings, albeit little portraiture. Prints and drawings were also auctioned, and during the wave of bankruptcies in the mid-1790s some fine examples of sculptural mantelpieces and quantities of exotic marbles came under the hammer.

••• See also **Horse and Carriage Sales**.

Backgammon

Rarely mentioned but certainly played, backgammon was the sole game the playwright John Gay had indulged in since arriving at Bath, so he told Swift in May 1728. Another visitor, Ned Ward, alluded in 1700 not just to backgammon but to 'Tick Tack', probably the variant on backgammon known better as 'trick track'. The game must have retained some popularity since shops were still advertising backgammon tables in 1771 and 1784.

Ballooning

The mania first infected Britain in 1783, soon after Montgolfier's successful ascents. That autumn saw the first of many copycat flights, manned and unmanned, right across the country, and by Christmas 1783 a certain Dinwiddie was exhibiting a small hydrogen balloon at Bath. On 10 January 1784 a crowd at the Riding School, Montpelier, watched it being laboriously filled with gas and then launched on what proved a 10-mile flight. In the event Dinwiddie had been narrowly forestalled by a hydrogen balloon constructed by a local physician, Dr C.H.Parry, which ascended two hours earlier and eventually came down somewhere beyond Wells, 19 miles away. Neither of these balloons carried any load. The notable balloonist Lunardi did exhibit a pretty-looking but viable passenger balloon at Gyde's Rooms in March 1785, but made his eventual ascent from Bristol. This left a Bath entrepreneur, James West, to promote his own intended manned flight, but in the end he scaled down his venture to two modest balloons, the largest only 13 feet across and not capable of carrying a person. These may have flown in May 1785. Aerostatic interest at Bath then faded until September 1802 when the experienced French balloonist (and pioneering parachutist) Garnerin made his well-publicised ascent, with a companion, from Sydney Gardens.

Balls see Assemblies and Assembly Rooms; Dancing.

Banquets

From time to time all kinds of groups and organisations dined at the various Bath inns - political parties, freemasons, Old Etonians, catch clubs, county societies, members of the Bath & West, to mention no more. These would usually be convivial sessions, gladdened by an appetising spread on the table, ample liquor, and dozens of much-applauded toasts. With some exceptions (such as ladies' nights held by the catch clubs) public dinners and suppers were wholly masculine affairs, a typical instance being the meal to honour George II's anniversary held in 1730 at Lindsey's newly opened Rooms - for which privilege some eighty male diners paid 19s.6d. apiece.

Putting all these in the shade were the grandest Guildhall banquets. The Corporation indulged in ordinary civic feasts several times a year. Each new Mayor was expected to provide one or more out of his stipend, as were the two Bailiffs from their profits on market rentals. Such feasts for the 31-man Corporation and guests must have been lavish enough, but they were quite outshone by the special banquets for royalty, or at certain election suppers, when every gastronomic stop was pulled. One of the finest banquets ever held in the old Stuart Guildhall marked the conferring of the city freedom on Frederick, Prince of Wales, in autumn 1738. Organised by the Earl of Chesterfield's own servants, it provided two main courses, each of 20-30 prepared dishes, and ended with 'the most elegant Des[s]ert that could Possibly be Procured', the entire junketing doubtless well lubricated with choice wines. A different Prince of Wales, the future George IV, who was similarly awarded his freedom, honoured the Corporations of Bath and Bristol jointly in 1796 with a sumptuous dinner at the (now Georgian) Guildhall, which the Corporation then reciprocated a few weeks later at the same place with a supper, preceded by a full-dress ball, for the royal dukes and 500 guests.

Since the Corporation oligarchy alone was responsible for choosing the city's two M.P.s and filling the office of Recorder, it was usual for successful candidates to repay their debt of gratitude with a Guildhall entertainment. Hence the ball and supper provided by the new Recorder, Thomas Potter, in 1758, or the banquet with which a later Recorder, Earl Camden, rewarded his electors and friends, seventy in all, in August 1794 - 'a dinner... at once profuse, elegant, and splendid', if rather noisy from the frequent cheers and acclamations. Eleazor Pickwick of the *White Hart* this time furnished the entire meal, no expense spared, down to the three turtles, the three fat bucks, and the excellent claret and Burgundy. Earlier banquets were often supplied by Phillott, landlord at the *Bear*, some of whose itemised bills in the City Chamberlain's records tell us just what was provided - including the 125 bottles of port, claret, Madeira, sherry, hock and cider that inaugurated R.P.Arden as a Bath M.P. in May 1794. Together with payments for musicians, waiters, porters, and a broken decanter, this bill topped £66. It can be compared with the huge sum of £125 expended on Abel Moysey's repast in 1792 after his swearing in as Recorder, the £30 dinner the Corporation permitted itself in June 1794 to salute Howe's great naval victory, and Phillott's £105 bill for the two mayoral feasts Walter Wiltshire awarded his colleagues on his taking office in 1791.

Bellringing

The peals that so often echoed through Bath were above all celebratory and loyalist. It is true that bells were rung for other purposes - the call to worship, the funeral knell, the signal for market trading to begin, or periodically in the seventeenth century to sound the alarm in case of fire. But the installation of eight bells in 1700 at the Abbey Church brought vastly new opportunities. The political implications became obvious during the attempted West Country rising of 1715 as the Abbey pealed joyfully to welcome a prominent Jacobite into Bath, but after this brief aberration the city's bells became deeply loyal and Hanoverian. For the rest of the century loud chiming hailed every coronation, dynastic marriage, royal birthday and wartime victory, reaching a crescendo when royalty actually visited the spa and the Corporation paid the bellringers to perform. Once the financial rewards became apparent, the ringers took to greeting every prominent new arrival with a merry round of bells, so that in high season the din was sometimes incessant. Persistent complaints about the 'cruel noise' and the torture inflicted on invalids date from at least 1721, when Lady Bristol called the bells the plague of her life. They had plenty of supporters nonetheless. St James's had its original eight bells re-cast in 1729, St Michael's hung eight more in 1758-9 (dispensing rum-and-brandy punch from the treble bell to celebrate the event), the Abbey increased its ring to ten, and even Walcot church talked of acquiring half-a-dozen. At St James's in 1753 Bath's Society of Ringers executed the first true full peal (5040 changes) to be rung in the west of England, and such was their prowess they loftily declined to compete at a striking competition on Twerton's euphonious bells in 1756 - 'The Gentlemen Ringers of Bath, being unwilling to discourage the County Ringers, are determined not to ring for the Prizes'. Occasional exploits in campanology aside, the bellringers still came in for much censure. But even the weighty appeal of the master-of-ceremonies in 1780 asking visitors not to encourage the ringers with tips proved largely useless. The performers found their hobby too lucrative to give up and in any case could always defend their jubilant pealing on national occasions as a patriotic duty. The composer Haydn noted in 1794 that the bells were heard mainly on Monday and Friday evenings, but that was in summer. In high season and times of war, Mrs Piozzi's words about them 'tolling every Day and all Day long' (February 1799) sound rather more typical.

Billiards

'Who'll play at Billiards... ?', asked some doggerel versifier in 1721. It was a well-established diversion, already in vogue at Bath in 1692 when the Prince of Denmark, Princess Anne's consort, amused himself at the billiard table there. For serious gamblers like the Earl of Abingdon, who lost heavily at the Bath tables in 1723, it provided a serious alternative to cards and dice, though in 1739 another confessed lover of 'deep play', the Earl of Chesterfield, took up the sticks or cues each morning, probably at the Assembly Rooms, solely 'for exercise'. Ralph Allen of Prior Park found billiards good for his health, and decades later the young artist Thomas Lawrence misspent some of his Bath youth honing his cueing skills. The game was significant enough locally by the 1740s to support a cabinet-maker with a special line in billiard tables, then as now covered in green baize and furnished with six pockets, but constructed without a slate bed. The best examples were in mahogany with carved mouldings. Advertisements in the 1750s suggest a good demand for billiards equipment from taverns, inns and coffee houses, and after 1771 the game flourished at the Upper Assembly Rooms which originally had an upstairs billiard room, then added a second, and finally built on a special annexe near the entrance. It was at one of the assembly rooms in 1780 that Edmund Rack watched a match played for considerable stakes - though hardly as high (in this public setting) as the £1000-£2000 bets cited by Smollett in his novel *Peregrine Pickle*, which includes a scene at some Bath billiard saloon in which a gang of sharpers are trounced at their own game.

    In real life the spa's reputation brought one of Europe's best players in 1799 to try his fortune. A former Dutch army officer, he enjoyed a very successful Bath run before being deported. (Might his arena have been the 'excellent and well-frequented Billiard-Room' then available at the Parade Coffee House?) Already the standard game was assuming its modern form, with the adoption of the completely straight cue and using three balls instead of two (which enabled scoring by cannons in addition to potting). Leather cue tips soon followed, and about 1820 Bath earned itself a notable niche in the annals of billiards with the famous innovation due to John Carr, professional at the Upper Assembly Rooms, of *chalking* the cue. This made screw shots feasible and Carr the national champion.

Boat Trips

Besides the utilitarian craft that plied the river - ferries, fishing boats, stone barges, and wherries carrying passengers and goods - there were pleasure boats to be hired. Samuel Tomkins, a Thames waterman, seems to have settled at Bath soon after the Avon Navigation had opened its through route to Bristol in 1727. It was he who conveyed Princess Amelia by wherry to Bristol and back in May 1728, and no doubt took the Prince and Princess of Wales to Saltford in 1750 for their riverside picnic. Other firms as well ran cargo and passenger vessels, but Tomkins was probably alone in having a dedicated pleasure boat available for hire. In 1740 he enlarged his small fleet with 'three new exceedingly neat and commodious Wherries, with a House on each, with Sash Windows, &c.', one of which was ready 'to be lett, at an Hour's Warning, to any select Company; being neatly ornamented, and designed for Expedition... [and] Mann'd with able London Watermen'. River transport above Bath remained hindered by weirs, so longer pleasure outings were necessarily downstream towards Saltford and beyond. Originally they most likely left from the *Packhorse*, or *Admiral Vernon* as Tomkins renamed it, beside Bath bridge, but in 1758 a flight of stone steps, Whitehall Stairs, was built down to the river at the end of South Parade to serve both a ferry service and Tomkins' pleasure boats. Later a small cabin under the stairs contained a popular exhibition of perspective views. It was perhaps from here that a boating party set out with a band of music (guitars, French horns, trumpets, etc.) one Sunday in June 1766 and gave offence for so desecrating the Sabbath. Messing about in boats may have been a commoner recreation than we imagine, though it was seldom spoken of in print. Spring Gardens, which bordered the river, advertised a pleasure craft for hire in 1766, and once Grosvenor Gardens had properly opened for business further upstream in 1793, rowing boats were certainly available on the nearby Avon at a shilling an hour - and this in addition to the Grosvenor ferry and the river-boat passenger service laid on from Bathwick directly to the Gardens.

Botanic Gardens

Little is known about the herb gardens that supplied Bath's numerous apothecaries, with one exception, William Sole's. An eminent botanist and author of standard works on English grasses and British mints, Sole partnered the apothecary Thomas West in Trim Street from c.1769 and established a private botanic garden just off the London Road. This was laid out on systematic Linnaean principles and could be visited by special appointment, as a group of high-ranking French courtiers did in 1787. Several years later a local amateur botanist and plant collector, John Jelly, a lawyer by profession, took over a nurseryman's garden (on what later became Prospect Place, Camden Road, but was then reached via Gay's Place) and called on Sole's expertise to help him design a public botanic garden. This opened to subscribers in September 1793 with coaxing words about the current vogue for botany and the importance to Bath of 'varying the Amusements'. In reality it proved an untimely venture. The market collapse brought on by the outbreak of war soon engulfed Jelly in huge property losses, and in April 1795 the garden, hothouse, moveable frames, and precious stock of plants were all up for auction after barely eighteen months on general view. Sole's own garden not only survived but in 1800 provided the specimens for a series of public botanical lectures. Other notable gardens of the period were sometimes privately shown - the Hon. Charles Hamilton's, for example, on the slopes behind the Royal Crescent - but though a number boasted rare and costly varieties they were aesthetically rather than scientifically laid out.

••• See also **Florists' Feasts**.

Bowling

Watched by an appreciative crowd of spectators, local bowlers won a famous match against the visitors in 1700, as the satirist Ned Ward vividly related. '*Fly, fly, fly, fly*, said one: *Rub, rub, rub, rub*, cry'd another. *Ten Guineas to five, I uncover the Jack*, says a third. *Damn these Nice Fingers of mine*, cry'd my Lord, *I slipt my Bowl, and mistook the Bias*. Another swearing he knew the Ground to an Inch, and would hold five Pound his Bowl came in. But in short, the Citizens won the Courtiers Money... '. This is recognisably the modern game, played with a target jack and weighted woods on no doubt close-cut turf. The venue would surely have been the spacious 'inner' bowling green lying below Gravel Walks just south-east of the Abbey Church. By tradition this was reserved for the gentry and had at times even served for country dancing. Other citizens made do until about 1677 with the rougher 'outer' green on the litton (i.e. the former churchyard) until this was superseded by a new bowling area west of St Michael's church. Both sites eventually fell prey to building speculators, the latter in 1716, when Green Street went up, and the gentry green in the late 1720s, apparently after a period of neglect, during the reconstruction of Terrace Walk and making of Lindsey's Rooms. Bowls suffered a national decline about this time, but it would be strange if the game lapsed altogether at Bath, given the opportunity it afforded for heavy betting under the pretext of taking healthy exercise. Still, it was not until the 1740s that a green was certainly in use in the old gardens between Harrison's (by then Simpson's) Rooms and the river. The bowling area at Spring Gardens may date from around the same time, though not securely documented until 1760. These remained Bath's principal greens until the 1790s when the two new pleasure gardens, Grosvenor and Sydney, both set aside generous space to devotees of bowling. This may well have stimulated fresh interest in the game, for in summer 1795, when Spring Gardens had scarcely three years left to run, it too put its green in order and re-opened to subscribers. There is no record of women playing at any point.

Boxing

Prizefighting was still admissible, even condoned, at Bath during the Coronation festivities of 1728, but like other lusty, crowd-pulling sports (wrestling, cudgelling, backsword) was eventually driven out for moral, economic and security reasons. Banned (1755 or earlier) from the strict confines of the city, it nonetheless continued to flourish outside, especially on that traditional day of working-class absenteeism 'Saint Monday'. Every Monday, ran one complaint in 1789, riotous boxing contests in the neighbourhood attracted idle, drunken crowds of spectators - to the detriment of both their employers and their families; and Sundays were little better, according to another account in 1797, as bare-knuckled local bruisers, stripped to the waist and urged on by 'horrid imprecations', slugged it out on Lansdown. There was a grudging admiration all the same. The 'Heroes of the Fist likewise made no small Part of each Day's Diversion', admitted the *Bath Journal* in 1760, reporting on a tournament otherwise devoted to backsword. And at Lansdown Fair in 1793 the *Bath Herald* fancied the spirit of Sir Bevil Grenvile must have wafted over from his nearby monument to inspire the combatants. Pugilism was always one of the Fair's attractions, with local fighters from Bath and Bristol much in evidence. But contests might be mounted at any time, given the backing of sporting gentry and keen betting on the result. Parfitt Maggs was their doughty Bath champion in the 1770s and the butcher Martin around 1790, while Charles Williams, a local locksmith, finally pummelled one Bristol opponent to a standstill in an unremitting two hours at Newton St Loe in 1798. A sparring match at the tennis court near the Riding School in October 1793 was no exception to the magistrates' long-standing local ban, since technically the site lay fractionally outside the city liberties. To keep the riffraff out and to pay for the event, it was in any case 'by subscription'.

Breakfasting

Joining a gregarious breakfast party - as often as not enlivened with music and dancing - could fill a morning in the way an assembly filled an evening. Like balls and theatre performances, the earlier breakfastings were always 'given', i.e. sponsored, generally by some leading figure among the spa visitors, occasionally by Nash or the proprietor of the Rooms. Originally held indoors in Harrison's Rooms or al fresco in the adjacent Harrison's Walks, breakfasting was mainly a spring and summer entertainment. As the visiting season evolved - to a point when the Rooms closed down during the summer months - the initiative gradually passed to the pleasure gardens which were geared up to serving light refreshments anyway.

Breakfastings were not casual. They were deliberately staged events, at set times, either public (organised and advertised by the garden proprietor) or private (ordered by some large party in advance). With time they became a highly efficient operation. A visitor in 1747 was impressed by the decorum of a concert breakfast he attended, the calm manner in which everyone was served with their choice. John Penrose's engaging *Letters from Bath* describes a private function at Spring Garden in 1766 for 17 Cornish gentry then staying at the spa - first the ferry crossing from Orange Grove, next the walk along gravel and grass walks to the long breakfast room with tables already laid, and then, at the word of command, the arrival of chocolate, coffee, tea, hot buttered rolls and hot Spring Garden cakes (Sally Lunns probably). This was a breakfasting *sans* music, but lines published in 1772 conjure up a full public occasion '... in a monstrous hot room, / Where we drink tea and choc'late, and eat

Sally Lum [*sic*]. / Our breakfast being over, away goes the table, / And we all dance Cotillions as well as we're able...'.

Twice-weekly public breakfastings were not cheap at 1s.6d. a head, but the cost did cover the band of music - at one time strings and wind (or hurdy-gurdy) but after c.1772 wind only (French horns and the newly fashionable clarinets). Cotillions and country dances sometimes went on until the early afternoon. Annually a full concert performance was given for the musicians' benefit. In hot weather there was a demand for musical afternoon teas, so Spring Gardens duly obliged with *thés dansants*. The profitability of breakfastings and teas encouraged other pleasure gardens to follow suit, the Bagatelle, King James's Palace, Bathwick Villa (which flew a flag on public days), and in the later 1790s Grosvenor and Sydney gardens. Occasionally they were held elsewhere. The old Harrison's Walks (now Gyde's) resounded once more to a public breakfasting, followed by a benefit wind band concert and cotillion dancing, one spring day in 1780, and a luxurious private breakfasting at Lansdown Grove in June 1799 merited a full account in the local press.

Cards

Usually played for money, cards ranked among the commonest eighteenth-century pastimes in all social circles, though only in the gambling centres of London's West End and spas like Bath did it regularly take on a compulsive, obsessive character. Card-games of different sorts had wide appeal, played equally at fashionable public tables, in low taverns, or quietly at home. 'Persons of all Characters and Denominations sit down to Cards from Morning to Night and Night to Morning...', ran one comment on Bath in 1737. They sat down at different times to Basset and Faro, Ombre and Quadrille, Piquet and Cribbage, Lasquenet and Commerce, Loo and Casino, and above all to Whist. Fortunes could be squandered all too readily at the prestigious old Venetian game of Basset and its variant Faro, both of which came under Parliamentary ban in 1739 together with Ace of Hearts, a game seen in action at Harrison's Rooms in 1725. Faro (or Pharaoh) appears to have been the most popular of the three at Bath. It required a special table painted with a suit of 13 cards on which bets were placed and against which the banker drew cards, one at a time, from a dealing box, with the odds constantly changing according to the order of the cards. The 'deep' players were bidding large sums at Bath's Faro tables in 1721 and the game still operated illegally much later in the century. In 1783 both Faro and EO, a kind of roulette, were played at one house, probably the one in Alfred Street to which John Twycross and Richard Wetenall, at their prosecution in 1787, were alleged to have lured 'unwary Country Gentlemen'.

Ombre, the preferred drawing-room game of the earlier eighteenth century, was, together with Quadrille, favoured especially by women according to a poem of 1734, Mary Chandler's *A Description of Bath* ('... fav'rite *Ombre*, sweetly sung by POPE // Appalls their *Cheeks* with *Fear*, or reddens them with *Hope*'). Subtle and entertaining, it was generally played in threesomes, one player against two, and required a pack of forty cards (the 8s, 9s and 10s discarded) and 'a great deal of Application'. Letters of the Countess of Bristol written from Bath in 1721 refer to her private Ombre party and in 1723 to playing modestly at 'three-penny ombre'. She also mentions tables for Commerce, a favourite adult pastime all through the century though eventually considered 'a dull round game' suitable only for children. Sarah Osborn took part in one-guinea Commerce at Bath in 1721, and twenty years later the bored bluestocking Elizabeth Montagu declared a 'pair royal' at Commerce the best excitement she could conjure up at the spa. Yet with its elements of barter and trading (as in later games like rummy and poker), the game was all the vogue and played for high stakes in the 1770s.

By the middle decades Whist was becoming a dominant force, and perhaps under its influence Quadrille, played in fours, supplanted the somewhat similar Ombre. Whist and Quadrille were still favourites at the Assembly Rooms in 1772, though one observer present noted that the Duchess of Northumberland's party was trying out the novel French game of Vingt-et-Un. Sheridan too mentioned the popularity of Quadrille with women. The fast-moving trumping game of Loo, which had a 3-card and a 5-card form, likewise featured sometimes at the Rooms - as in October 1766 when the Duchess of Bedford encouraged Loo parties every evening (while Horace Walpole stayed at his lodgings and stuck to quiet Cribbage). Lansquenet (from the German 'Landsknecht') was also having a vogue at this period to judge from Christopher Anstey's *New Bath Guide*. But Whist had most adherents of all. As early as 1725 we hear of one visitor whiling away the hours at Whist with his Bath landlady and two maids, and Whist was the card game Lord Chesterfield turned to in 1739. This antedated the publication of Hoyle's famous *Short Treatise on... Whist* in 1742, reprinted at Bath in 1743, which not only codified the rules but gave numerous examples of playing for advantage (and subsequently did the same for Quadrille and Piquet). From then on Whist (or Whisk) never lost favour. We find the Duke of Bedford sitting down each evening to 'Guinea Whisk' in 1746, and many people at the Rooms in 1747 watching the play of Whist rather than the spin of the EO ball. In 1780 one witness called Whist 'the only fashionable game' at assemblies and noted the packs of cards on sale at the Rooms. Even Casino, a card game of real skill popular from the 1790s, or another favourite, Pope Joan, would not dislodge Whist.

In 1777 the popularity of cards had induced the proprietors of the Upper Assembly Rooms to add on an extra card room. Edmund Rack looked in one day in 1780 and noted '17 Card Tables full [and] Gold & Notes to Considerable Amount on each'. But the old plague of routs - card parties held at private houses - badly damaged custom at the public rooms throughout the 1780s and 1790s and was condemned to little effect. 'Only went to two plays and one dress-ball', ran a typical comment in 1796, 'but card-parties impossible to escape...'. The professional gamblers, resident or visiting, were another scourge, and the century closed with warnings that Faro and Hazard specialists could be expected from London.

••• See also **Gambling; Routs.**

Carriage Drives see **Riding and Carriage Drives.**

Catch Clubs

Taking their cue from the Noblemen's and Gentlemen's Catch Club founded in London in 1761, music societies for male voices gradually became established in other towns. Typically their meetings included a good supper preceded by the singing of catches and glees - contrapuntal and harmonic part-songs that covered many moods but inclined to the comic, bibulous, dramatic, patriotic, and sweetly sentimental. At Bath in the late 1770s part-singers sometimes competed for a silver cup, and from c.1782 a catch club, Bath Musical Society, was meeting weekly at the *Raven* in Abbey Green and occasionally performing at concerts elsewhere and at the pleasure gardens. A new phase began in 1786 with the birth of a more socially select institution, the New Musical Society or Bath Catch Club, at the *White Lion* inn. It was convivial but decorous, with a presiding chairman for each meeting and most of the subscribing gentry content to listen rather than perform at the rather high musical standard expected. Among the fine singers in the late 1780s was the up-and-coming celebrity tenor, Charles Incledon, one of several participants from the Bath Theatre. Boy trebles may have performed, as they did at public concerts, but no female voices, though the occasional elegant ladies' nights held at the Guildhall from January 1787 onwards enabled subscribers to introduce women guests and sometimes swelled the audience to c.300.

In the highly charged political atmosphere of the 1790s the Bath Catch Club plunged into controversy by dismissing its secretary for suspected radicalism, and then in December 1795, facing financial losses, suspended its activities - only to be resurrected almost at once in the shape of the loyalist Bath Harmonic Society under the respected leadership of the former Mayor and spirited composer of catches, Dr Henry Harington. Now meeting at the *White Hart*, but appropriating the Lower Assembly Rooms for its socially unmissable ladies' nights, the Harmonic Society reached a zenith of polite acceptability when the Prince of Wales himself joined in April 1799. Its chief performers had brought glee-singing to some sort of perfection. It surpassed every rival, thought the *Bath Herald*, 'in the delights of harmony and rationality' and was the most sought-after, well-regulated and splendid institution of its kind in the country.

Chess

So various was chess, explained Richard Seymour in *The Compleat Gamester* (5th ed. 1734), that even if they play for nothing people still find it absorbing 'which can hardly be said of any other Game'. Is this why chess was little cultivated in eighteenth-century Bath, because it lacked the element of chance, because the titillation of the wager was missing?

Church- and Chapel-going

For all the hedonism and worldliness of Bath, religion was a serious matter to the many guests and citizens who worshipped regularly and would pack the pews to hear a noted preacher. In addition, and hence their mention here, places of worship offered entertainment of a kind. Sightseers included them in their itineraries about town, for example. The Abbey Church was visited for its architecture and monuments. The other parish churches provoked less tourist curiosity than the various proprietary chapels - from the shockingly cosy drawing-room interior of the Octagon in Milsom Street to the pinnacled All Saints' on Lansdown. In the later 1760s and 1770s no religious institution fascinated outsiders more than the Countess of Huntingdon's chapel in Vineyards. Titled patronage, elegant trappings, and hell-fire preaching together made a combination so irresistible that attendance at services had for a period to be controlled by ticket. Even those who mocked the pulpit oratory were usually seduced by the hymn singing - 'slow, solemn, sweet and affecting to a great degree' in the words of one witness - and generally reckoned superior to the efforts of the Charity School children at the Abbey Church. The latter, however, owned a fine Jordan organ that Thomas Chilcot inaugurated in 1740 with a grand instrumental concert. This foreshadowed many notable choral performances in later years at the Abbey in aid of the Hospital and Sunday School charities, as it did the less-frequent oratorios put on at the Octagon, St James's, and elsewhere. Otherwise the Abbey Church was the scene of notable civic spectacle at Mayor-makings, charity sermons, national thanksgivings, and the like.

Circulating Libraries

Unlike book clubs and learned subscription libraries, circulating libraries were commercial enterprises, usually run in tandem with bookshops as a means of stimulating business at a period when printed publications were relatively expensive items. Given the presence at the spa of so many invalids and visitors with time to kill, it was natural for Bath to have tried them early. James Leake, reared in the London book trade, succeeded to Henry Hammond's Bath bookshop in 1721/22 and soon began to rent out books from his ideally sited premises, jutting forward on Terrace Walk almost opposite Harrison's Rooms. In no time Leake's was a celebrated Bath institution, its walls lined with mirrors and tall bookshelves, frequented in the season by the *beau monde* of both sexes - as avid for news and gossip as on exchanging loans. By making available newspapers and space for conversation, circulating libraries to some extent aped the coffee-houses - with one of which Leake was directly associated through his daughter, married to the master of the Grove Coffee-house. Brother-in-law to the novelist Richardson, Leake was also close to the Ralph Allen/ Dr Cheyne circles - connections which earned him a tremendous puff in the 1742 edition of Defoe's *Travels* as 'one of the finest Bookseller's shops in Europe'.

Although Leake's was the best known, other libraries were established over the years by William Frederick, Benjamin Matthews, Thomas Mill, William Taylor, and William Bally - all before 1770, the date at which Leake's son sold the Terrace Walk library to Lewis Bull, under whom it continued to thrive until the end of the century. Bull 'hates the very Sight of me...', Mrs Piozzi once confessed, 'because I come to his Shop at 8 or 9 o'Clock in the Morning... the only Leisure hour the Man has from Readers who sit round his Table all Noon and Footmen who ferret after him for Novels all Night'. Mrs Piozzi was after serious reading, not novels, but the libraries could supply literature of every kind and in half-a-dozen languages, from literary classics, history, science and religion to erotica, plays, political tracts and even books for children.

Subscribing to one of the libraries ought to be a priority for families staying at Bath, one writer advised in 1782, and some went further - a certain Elizabeth Collett and her niece, for example, who spent eleven weeks at the spa in 1792, subscribed to four. At that date there were around eight libraries to choose from, all operating a common charging policy, among them Bull's, Meyler's in Orange Grove, Hazard's in Cheap Street, and Pratt & Marshall's at the top of Milsom Street. In 1793 the latter library alone had more than 500 subscribers, while its records over the next seven years listed no fewer than 188 titled nobility and gentry, 144 military and naval officers, and 121 clerics, even though it was then losing business to rivals. Several libraries tempted customers by opening newspaper rooms. Samuel Hazard's was carpeted, kept warm by a fire, looked out over the churchyard, and kept a large selection of current newspapers (35 of them provincial or Irish) and this in addition to the stock of over 10,000 volumes for loan in the library downstairs. The circulating library principle had long since spread to other cultural areas. Rickards' printshop in [Old] Bond Street was as ready to hire out engravings as the music dealer Lintern in the Churchyard was to lend his customers music scores and instruments.

Circus

Equestrian circus acts reached Bath at a relatively early date thanks to its riding schools, or specifically to Samuel Ryle's Riding School, established in winter 1787-88 at his livery stables on Monmouth Street. The impetus (and possibly some of the capital) for the venture stemmed from his links with the rival London circus- and riding-masters Philip Astley and Charles Hughes. From the start Ryle had his riding arena roofed over to create a seated amphitheatre on the metropolitan model, lit by oil-lamps and soon to be warmed by stoves. Here the entertainment of circus, still a novelty outside London, was launched in February-April 1788 with eye-opening feats of horsemanship and acrobatics and to musical accompaniment. The star of the show was Benjamin Handy, 'the vaulting horseman', but the team of nine performers included rope-dancers and a child of 30 months. If the riding-master Thomas Franklin missed this trial run, he certainly came with the troop in December 1788 on the first of their many return visits. Lengthy press announcements give a good impression of the stunts performed - among them a hornpipe danced on a galloping horse, vaulting by Handy while bound and blindfold, high-level tumbling, trampoline tricks, and a comic 'Ride to Brentford'. Except for the staging of a mock sea fight and storm at the Amphitheatre by an Italian company in 1793-94, Handy's and Franklin's equestrians continued to include Ryle's on their annual tours for almost a decade, keeping their programme fresh with a string of innovations - from Russian performers one year to an actual foxhunt, pony racing, pantomime acts, and even fireworks. Tragically, Handy's troop was reported lost crossing the Irish Sea in January 1798. Ryle at once gave up promoting equestrian diversions, leaving the field to Perry's Circus which opened at a newly erected amphitheatre in Frog Lane (location of the future New Bond Street) in 1800.

Cockfighting

The sport was organised periodically in and around Bath itself as well as being widespread in the countryside. As a rule the town events were challenge matches between local counties held over two to three days at the cockpit of a designated inn, for example Gloucestershire versus Somerset in 1725 and Herefordshire and Gloucestershire versus Dorset in 1729, one at the *White Lion*, the other at the *Lamb* (the former cockpit in Timber Green having fallen out of use by then). The *Lamb* staged the majority of encounters in the 1730s-1740s and always provided an 'ordinary' (i.e.a set-price meal) for the participants. The birds, specially trained by their 'feeders' and spurred for battle, would be officially weighed a day or so before fighting. Each side entered an agreed number, typically 31 or 41 cocks for the main bouts at 4 guineas per battle, 10 for the 2-guinea by-battles, and several more for odd 40-guinea battles. Occasionally an individual breeder would supply all the cocks for one side, as Richard Champneys did in 1744 for a match against breeders from Bath and Wells. Cockfights attracted a good attendance of country gentry and betting must have been fierce and vociferous. After the mid-century however, as the sport grew less fashionable under the accusation of being uncivilised, it retreated from central Bath to the outskirts. Even so, as late as 1798 Somerset and Wiltshire gentry fought a main of cocks over two days near Grosvenor Gardens. This was more than four decades after the Bath magistrates had first tried to stop the brutalising annual custom of Throwing at Cocks (for which see **Popular Sports**).

Coffee-houses

Proliferating as they did in Restoration London, coffee-houses were soon imitated elsewhere. Bath certainly had one by 1679, probably at the sign of the Turk's Head in the Marketplace. Under Robert Sheyler this moved c.1694 to new premises at the upper corner of Cheap Street, where it continued under Elizabeth and Robert Sheyler junior until sometime after 1718. By then a second coffee-house - Benjoy's/Bengy's (after its proprietor Benjamin Jellicot) - had arisen at the south end of Terrace Walk, usefully adjacent to the bowling green, but this eventually fell victim to Wood's redevelopment scheme c.1728. In 1720-1 Thomas Sheyler gave a fresh fillip to Bath's fashionable quarter near Gravel Walks, the future Orange Grove, by opening a coffee-house on a strategic corner site at the exit of an intended pedestrian way (Wade's Passage) from Abbey Churchyard. In a short time it was an indispensable institution.

As genteel places to eat and drink, to meet one's social peers, and to catch up on news, coffee-houses met several needs at once, and did so by charging a subscription for their use. This distanced them from public taverns and kept the company reasonably select. Equally it allowed them to provide a congenial milieu, a range of current newspapers and other publications, and free use of writing materials. Licensed to sell alcohol as well as hot drinks and snacks (rolls, Bath buns, soups, savoury jellies, syllabubs), and often indeed run by ex-wine-and-brandy merchants, coffee-houses above all did duty as male clubs. In London particular interest groups tended to congregate at particular coffee-houses. At Bath, with far fewer such institutions, all parties mingled. The majority of subscribers would be visiting gentry, for the coffee-house offered a temporary headquarters, acceptable company, and certain basic facilities - such as a place to eat breakfast for those staying in lodgings. The Grove Coffee-house, where Charles Morgan succeeded Thomas Sheyler c.1731, enjoyed a virtual 20-year monopoly once Benjoy's, its only rival, had gone, and in 1733 it managed to thwart John Wood's plan to extend the Pump Room on the grounds that this might damage the coffee-house trade. Several hundred subscribed each season, including many notabilities. Viscount Percival, for example, mentions in his diary taking part in various instructive debates on political, religious and literary topics at the Grove in 1730 in the company of the Speaker of the House of Commons, a high court judge (Sir Edmund Probyn), the Dean of Exeter, and others.

As the numbers of affluent spa visitors built up and the season steadily lengthened, a second coffee-house opened in 1750 close to the old site of Benjoy's, at the busy pedestrian junction of Terrace Walk and North Parade. The building belonged to the silk mercers J & P Ferry, who shared the premises with the coffee-house for another year or two before removing. It may have been then that the billiard room was added and a 'marker' appointed to keep the score, advantages the Grove Coffee-house apparently never had and which may have cost it custom. A wine-merchant, Richard Stephens, held the Parade Coffee-house 1755-67, followed in fairly quick succession by Robert Boulter, William Mackclary and Peter Temple, before Meshach Pritchard, another local wine merchant, took control 1776-99 - during part of which time he also managed Spring Gardens. At the Grove Coffee-house this long tenure was matched by George Frappell, master 1771-96, who died just as he branched out into a new venture, George's Coffee-house near the Pump Room.

Competition stepped up noticeably in the last third of the century. In the upper town the provision of a coffee room at the new York House hotel in 1769 was followed in 1771 by another at the Upper Assembly Rooms, which was capped within a year by the decision to build on an annexe coffee room beside the front entrance to the Rooms. These amenities serving the population of lower Lansdown were supplemented in 1796 by St James's Coffee-house behind Royal Crescent. In the same way the Argyle coffee-house and tavern (near Pulteney Bridge, from 1790) and the coffee room at Sydney Gardens (by 1798) catered to the needs of developing Bathwick. The fast-expanding local economy of these years also ushered in a subtly different style of coffee room more geared to business interests and commercial travellers, examples being the rooms opened at the *Christopher*, *Angel* and *Castle* inns (1763, 1782 and 1799 respectively), the Bath Coffee-house in Stall Street (1770-79),

City Coffee-house in the Marketplace (1799-1800), and the coffee room for 'respectable tradesmen' at Spring Gardens in 1795.

The Ladies' Coffee-house was far more unusual, a phenomenon possibly unique to Bath, certainly in its longevity. It may have started with a toyshop offering its female customers refreshments and newpapers - sometime before 1740 when the bluestocking Elizabeth Montagu complained of having to hear about everyone's ailments there. By 1755 it seems to have stood on the east side of the Pump Room forecourt, managed by Elizabeth Taylor (of the adjoining jeweller's) and Clementine Foord. In the 1760s and 1770s it was on the opposite side, next-but-one to the Pump Room. Lydia Melford in Smollett's tongue-in-cheek fiction *Humphry Clinker* remarks that young women like her were banned from attending because 'the conversation turns upon politics, scandal, philosophy, and other subjects above our capacity'. A lecture on the art of speaking was given there in June 1773 at the time of Richard and Ann Immins' short occupancy, but the room was then let once more and this intriguing institution may not have survived much longer - though a certain Mary Hamilton, lodging in May 1774 in Milsom Street, does record taking breakfast at a coffee-house, perhaps this one.

Concerts

Performances to be listened to, as distinct from the street medleys of the City Waits or the morning mood music supplied by the Pump Room band, were rather haphazard features of earlier spa life. They depended largely on well-known musicians turning up or being invited from London, and on wealthy patrons and amateur devotees then sponsoring recitals for their friends. In September 1709 the company were being 'highly entertained with Singing and Musick, by the famous Nicoleno & Valentinio [Nicolini & Valentini]', and such Italian virtuosi probably paid regular visits between their metropolitan engagements. The violinist-composer Geminiani came in 1718, and mention once more of the great castrato Nicolini - 'Here's half a Guinea / To hear *Nicolini*' - suggests that some concerts may already have been financed in series by subscription. By the 1730s and 1740s a Music Society of Bath was in existence where good amateur players took part alongside resident professionals (from the Pump/Assembly Rooms band, the theatre, and perhaps the City Waits). Performances were given at the Assembly Rooms and presumably at Wiltshire's so-called 'Concert Room' on Terrace Walk. 'We have had morning concerts here lately', Elizabeth Montagu wrote in January 1741, adding that 'most of the performers were gentlemen'. Bath's professional musicians, led by the violinist Francis Fleming and the Abbey Church organist Thomas Chilcot, faced increasing high-season competition from Italian singers and instrumentalists in the 1740s-1750s, culminating around 1755-8 in open clashes with the visiting impresario Giuseppe Passerini, who brought his own musicians from London as well as exploiting those at Bath. In defiance of Passerini a much-praised *Acis & Galatea* was given by some forty performers at Simpson's Rooms in 1757. A still more valuable initiative, the prestigious Hospital charity concerts at the Abbey Church, largely Handelian in character, also date from this period.

The young bass singer and harpsichord-player, Thomas Linley, was now coming to the fore. Shouldering his rivals aside, he eventually took charge of the concerts (nominally under the master-of-ceremonies) on his own account. Though the violinists Fleming and David Richards retained their benefit concerts, and visiting musicians periodically staged other performances, it was Linley who now organised the principal subscription series and who in 1771 was appointed musical director at the new Upper Rooms. Meanwhile William Herschel had appeared on the scene and for a time collaborated with Linley, but as a busy music tutor, concert-master at Spring Gardens, and organist at the Octagon chapel, also cultivated his own clientèle. His staging of Handel's *Messiah* at the Octagon in 1770 nevertheless demonstrated his independence, and two years later, after a dispute with Linley, he defected to the Lower Rooms, so aggravating the divisions between the two Rooms over their respective support for Pump Room music. The split brought several years of rival concert promotions, rival oratorios, and rival benefit performances, through all of which Linley wielded one undeniable trump card in his highly musical family, especially the angelic soprano Elizabeth Linley, a star attraction at any concert. In winter 1777-78 he directed his final Bath season, having already removed to London with at least the satisfaction of knowing that in a nearly twenty-year reign he had raised performance standards at the spa and introduced a much more varied repertoire, including preclassical symphonic music with its new forms and textures and greater need for precision.

Ever more absorbed by astronomy, Herschel in his last years at Bath mainly concentrated on oratorio. Before he left in 1781 concert promotion was in fresh hands. In 1777-80 the main programme was under the newcomer Franz Lamotte, but thereafter his close collaborator, Venanzio

Rauzzini, took control. Already a highly popular castrato singer with spa audiences, Rauzzini proved an inspired concert director. Over the next two decades and against all financial odds, the concerts went musically from strength to strength. His wide contacts enabled him to lure a wonderful galaxy of metropolitan and international talents to Bath, some of them even waiving their fees out of friendship and respect. Season after season audiences were treated to the finest performers - the female singers Mara, Billington, Negri, Storace and Mountain; the male singers Tenducci, Braham, Harrison, Rovedino and Kelly; and such great instrumentalists as the violinists Pieltain, Giornovicchi and Janiewicz, double-bass Dragonetti, oboist Fischer, and the pianist-composers J.B.Cramer and Dussek; and all these in addition to a number of Bath artists who also shone - the soprano Anne Cantelo, the brilliant pianist Jenny Guest, and the flautist Arthur Ashe, to name no more.

The repertoire was equally ambitious, with Handel, as ever, heading the list of 'ancient' favourites and Haydn the modernist school. Programmes were often in fact divided into two stylistic halves, baroque items followed by *galant*/classical compositions, and the whole well interspersed with Italian and English vocal music, in an attempt to satisfy all tastes. Besides the 8-, 10- or 12-concert subscription series (constantly teetering on the brink of financial collapse), there were dozens of competing individual concerts - ranging from recitals by child prodigies (like the astonishing black violinist Bridgtower in 1789) to the instrumental and vocal divertissements at the pleasure gardens and the Lent/Easter oratorios at the Rooms or, on occasion, the theatre. Private concerts flourished as well. The Sunday evening concerts at the house of Rauzzini's greatest admirer, Miss Wroughton, were matched in quality only by the magical impromptus at Rauzzini's own Perrymead villa, where in 1794 even the great Haydn found himself engaged.

••• See also **Breakfasting; Catch Clubs; Pleasure Gardens; Pump Room; Theatre; Waits Music.**

Cricket

Perhaps around the mid-century, soon after the game had been codified but still in the era of two-stump wickets and underarm bowling, cricket spread to the Bath locality from its early stronghold in the south-east. A speculative match in memory of the Prince of Wales took place at Saltford meadow in July 1751, and in due course cricket established itself on Claverton Down - witness a one-day match played there in October 1768 for a 22-guinea prize. The patrons would have been visiting enthusiasts to judge by the late-season date. By 1782 a rather casual Bath Cricket Club had been formed, but organised only one official game each year. Cricket gradually acquired a local following and became a popular enough pastime to be specifically banned as a disturbance, along with quoits, from Bathwick Meadows in 1792. Even so, the *Bath Chronicle* in 1795 still thought regular matches on Claverton Down rather a novelty.

Dancing

This was among the best-liked of all Georgian social recreations, especially by women. But learning to dance had a more fundamental rationale than simply preparing for the ballroom, since it was thought to polish manners, teach graceful deportment, and assist the acquisition of that air of unstudied ease so much admired in well-bred society. Dancing-masters and dancing-mistresses consequently flourished at Bath, a place where scrutiny in the drawing-room could be as intense as scrutiny at the ball. The ball was nonetheless the ultimate showpiece, and no spotlight exposed the participants so thoroughly as the solo minuet.

A dress ball in its purest format comprised two distinct parts with a supper interlude. Part one was wholly devoted to French dances. Early in the century the *rigaudon* was still danced, and perhaps the *bourée* and stately *courant* as well, but by the 1720s the minuet alone seems to have been admissible, executed by a single couple at a time under the critical gaze of the assembled company. Couples stood up in order of precedence, each male dancer taking two successive female partners - a means of disguising the relative lack of willing males (which sometimes obliged the master of ceremonies to take to the floor himself). How long the succession of minuets took depended on the number of dancers who came forward, but it could be tedious for the onlookers, especially if watching mediocre performers. The whole ritual survived so long only because it was loaded with the symbolism of Court etiquette. Not only had the repeating figures, movements and graces of the minuet to be accomplished with precision and finesse, the dancers were also differentiated by extra formality of costume ('an essential Point of Decorum', it was emphasised), i.e. full-trimmed dress for both sexes, lappets and large hoops for women, and bag-dressed wig for men. Once the second part of the programme, the country dances, began, the position was reversed: lappets and hoops were then specifically ruled unacceptable (and had to be removed in the changing area). These were longways dances that anyone might join in. They were performed in rows of facing couples, with dancing down the rows from top to bottom and many hopping steps and chaining patterns. Precedence was observed only as the rows were being formed. The top couple ranked highest and 'called the tune', but then danced down the row to the bottom. '*Country dance*, of all others, best pleases the fair', was a common refrain, and it was this informal style of dance that was always preferred outside the ballroom proper, at pleasure gardens, say, or private receptions.

About 1770 a new vogue hit Bath, the cotillion, brought from Paris, tried out first at Spring Gardens, then introduced at the Assembly Rooms in winter 1770-71. Danced in sets of four couples, this was a *contredanse*, a formalised English country dance in effect, akin to the allemande which arrived about the same time. Cotillion balls vied with dress balls at Bath for the remainder of the century, and since they allowed more participation, offered more variety, and were less stuffy about dress, they were generally more popular. But even the minuets were affected by the greater numbers now attending balls and by major changes in dress fashions. The politician John Wilkes noticed in 1778 that minuets were already being danced three couples at a time to speed the process, and by the 1780s the minuet had been hybridised with the longways to produce the 'long minuet' that usually ended the ball. Meanwhile the old dress distinctions were disappearing, so that for minuets lappets alone remained *de rigueur*, and at 'fancy balls' almost any decent costume was allowed. In the 1790s, during a sudden Romantic flush of interest in things Celtic, Scottish reels and strathspeys and even Irish jigs also invaded the balls, and by 1800 the triple-time rhythms of the daring Viennese waltz were being heard in the dancing masters' rooms. What was danced at Bath influenced other places, for visitors took home with them not just memories but also tangible proofs in the shape of booklets recording the steps and tunes of the season's dances. The local names that many were given ensured that 'Beechen Cliff', 'Orange Grove', 'Lady Pulteney' and many more continued to echo around the kingdom, adding another glow to the spa's reputation.

Supporting the ball rituals was the tuition of the dancing instructor, whose capabilities could be publicly demonstrated towards the end of the century in glamorous pupils' balls. Particularly under the highly admired dancing mistress Anna Fleming, these virginal displays drew crowds of onlookers (including the Prince of Wales himself in 1799) to observe upwards of fifty children and adolescent schoolgirls, uniformly gowned in muslin, going through their expensively acquired paces in figure dances and group minuets. The local press was regularly of the opinion that a sweeter, more fairylike spectacle could scarcely be conceived.

••• See also **Assemblies and Assembly Rooms**; **Breakfasting**; **Festivities** [for reference to Morris Dancing]; **Pleasure Gardens**.

Dice

In a play scene of c.1725, set in a Bath gaming room, a furious noblewoman is stripped of all her money at dice. It reflected reality. Greater sums were sometimes risked on the roll of the dice than on any other diversion - never mind if a single bad throw, as one observer put it, was likely to sour the blood more than ten glasses of spa water could ever sweeten it. There was no conversation at Bath, Lady Orkney complained in 1711, because the rattling dice took all the company's attention. Several different games were played. Two local operators, John and Philip Ditcher, were each fined two guineas in 1713 for allowing sets of eight illegally marked dice to be used in 'one New Invention alias a Fair Chance, with Forty Eight Chances', not a game that caught on widely. The evidence suggests habitual dicers liked Hazard best, 'a game that makes a man or undoes him in the twinkling of an eye'. More 'bewitching' than simply throwing for doublets (the procedure in common dice games like Passage), Hazard could be played by any number at a time, being a contest between a single caster (the bank) and the rest, and the outcome depending on the 'mains', 'chances', and 'nicks' scored by two dice. The Countess of Bristol deigned to play Hazard for unusually low stakes in August 1721 'for most of the ladys play silver', but three weeks later, betting having improved, won £50 by throwing 15 mains one morning. Over £2500 in modern values, this was still a modest win set against the 'very deep play' that a recently arrived set of gambling noblemen were then engaged in. For reckless and inexperienced gamblers dicing could be truly hazardous: falsely numbered or loaded dice were but samples of the armoury stacked against them. The third Duke of Bedford for one might have lost a fortune to a crooked gambling syndicate at Bath if Beau Nash, himself in the know, had not intervened. As abuses mounted, Parliament finally outlawed Hazard in 1739 and other games of dice a year later. Roulette-type games were soon introduced to circumvent the ban, but in private illicit (and rigged) dicing went on anyway. In fact the *Bath Chronicle* took the trouble in 1789 tell its readers exactly how cheating with false dice was accomplished.

••• See also **Gambling**.

Duelling

While hardly an entertainment for those directly concerned, duelling deserves mention because contests originated most often in gambling disputes. The duel in 1705 that killed the gamester Captain Webster, Bath's first master-of-ceremonies, had this cause, as did a subsequent torchlit combat in Orange Grove between two gamesters, Taylor and Clarke, in which Taylor was severely wounded. Such violent episodes were quite contrary to Beau Nash's scheme for spa harmony and probably inspired his crusade against the carrying of swords. This still left pistols, the weapons preferred in the duel over a billiards debt between Charles

Jones and Bazil Prise in 1731, Bath being put 'in great confusion' when
Prise, son of a Bath merchant, was shot dead and Jones absconded. That
meeting took place in Harrison's Walk, but another duel in 1729 had
favoured Claverton Down and in future most contests would be held in
privacy out of town.

Around the middle decades duelling fell out of fashion but revived
about 1770. Sheridan's famous two encounters with Matthews over
Elizabeth Linley date from this time. The first took place indoors in
London, but Kingsdown was chosen for the second in July 1772, fought
with swords and leaving Sheridan with a near-fatal wound. The dawn
pistol duel in 1778 between the vicomte du Barré and his hitherto close
companion comte Rice was fought near Claverton racecourse. Rice,
himself injured in the groin, killed the vicomte with his second shot, the
inquest bringing in a verdict of manslaughter and the vicomte's grave at
Bathampton becoming a pilgrimage spot for years to come. Public
fascination with duels was fanned again in 1780 by the Brereton-Spooner
quarrel. In a drunken stupor Spooner had lost £2000 gambling with the
notorious George Brereton, son of the master-of-ceremonies. Brereton
reneged on a promise not to press the debt until Spooner's father died;
insults and challenges were exchanged; the pair had to be forcibly
separated in the Assembly Rooms; and in the ensuing pistol fight (held
near Prior Park) Spooner was badly hurt, and Brereton made his escape
amid widespread condemnation. The magistrates managed to avert
another gamesters' duel in 1789, but duelling remained deeply ingrained
in patrician and military culture. Further down the social scale most
ordinary male disputes would be settled in backstreet fistfights, so that
when a barber and a baker jumped class and faced each other with pistols
at Widcombe in 1783, the *Bath Journal* treated the whole business, which
ended without injury, as rather a joke.

EO

Otherwise written E & O, OE, or in its full form Evens and Odds, EO
was one of several games on the roulette principle invented c.1740 to
replace dice. After successful testing at Tunbridge Wells, EO spread to
Bath when Nash installed a £15 table at each of the Assembly Rooms
(but much later, in 1754-55, would sue both Rooms for being cheated of
his EO profits). 'Table' was rather a misnomer for what was in fact a
shallow bowl containing a balanced wheel, neatly crafted in mahogany
and brass and hinting of a ship's compass, in which a small ball was

allowed to spin before dropping into one of 40 slots alternately lettered E or O. Betting was simplicity itself, for or against the likelihood of the ball entering an E or O slot. It was, thought one visitor, Joseph Draper, in 1747 a ridiculous occupation, yet with both sexes it was all the rage at Bath, and Draper noticed even a bishop watching the play. The game was nevertheless banned by Parliament from 1750 and the Bath magistrates acted at once. In January 1750 they arrested a dozen or more gamesters at a house near Westgate and made a bonfire of their EO table. The same autumn they descended on several other EO houses that had sprung up since. For a time the game remained suppressed, but in the late 1770s 'those abominable engines of fraud' regained their popularity and EO tables once more arrived surreptitiously at Bath. In 1781 one operated in Orchard Street until seized, and the magistrates had two others publicly burned in 1783. This had some effect. The next records of EO tables in the Bath neighbourhood date from the later 1790s when they were set up annually at Lansdown Fair.

　•••　See also **Gambling**.

Excursions see **Boat Trips**; **Rambling**; **Riding and Carriage Drives**.

Exhibitions

Temporary shows, displays and demonstrations were less predictable than the standard round of amusements and took many forms. Some originated at Bath, but many more came from London and elsewhere on travelling circuits through the West Country. The 'Microcosm' is a good example, toured repeatedly around Britain from the 1740s. A large and ingenious contraption, part work of art, part miniature theatre with moving figures, part musical box, part planetarium, it first intrigued Bath audiences in winter 1747-48, returned in 1757 and again in 1773, when this 'matchless pile of art' went through its transformation scenes four times a day. Mechanical devices were always popular. In 1754 and 1769 the different stages of the Norfolk worsted cloth manufacture could be seen acted out by 18-inch figures in over 3000 clockwork movements. A similar spectacle in 1760 attracted Mrs Delany who discovered 'a curious machine, that represents the whole progress of working the copper and silver and gold mines in Saxony'. For several seasons (1780-83) one enterprising showman brought to Bath a collection of Thomas Jervais glass paintings, mostly copies of old masters and full of striking lighting effects, to which he added other dramatic transparencies hugely magnified and a further optical show involving a camera obscura, De Loutherbourg's eidophusikon, and background music. Optical devices like the camera obscura (a large one standing in Sydney Gardens in 1795), travelling peepshows, *ombres chinoises*, mobile panoramas of sea battles and the like, had an almost guaranteed success. So too did waxworks which reached Bath in 1728, 1748, 1759, 1762, 1779, and culminated in Mrs Sylvester's 'Royal Waxwork' of 1796, comprising 36 lifesize figures, shown for eleven hours a day at a room in Orange Grove and said to be constantly crowded with spectators. Parrot's rock shellwork in 1751 likewise proved a good draw, a foretaste of later displays of shells, fossils and similar natural curiosities, or the mock-natural specimens seen in the 'Grand Artificial Flower Garden' laid out in the former Assembly Rooms on Terrace Walk in late 1781, with room for over seventy visitors at a time to stroll among 4000 simulated plants, shrubs and trees.

Two further exhibitions were rich in local appeal - rival wooden models of contemporary Bath, one built by the portrait-painter Joseph Sheldon at a scale of 1:300, the other by the surveyor-architect Charles Harcourt Masters at 1:360. Minutely detailed (down to glazing in the windows of the miniature buildings), both models went on public view at Bath by 1789 and and later in London. Removable buildings from Masters' lay-out were even shown to George III at Weymouth. Other architectural models appeared from time to time but none held the fascination of these Lilliputian townscapes.

••• See also **Artists' Exhibitions and Studios; Auctions; Guildhall; Menageries; Window-shopping**.

Fairs and Revels

In origin fairs were great occasional markets for selling animals, agricultural produce, and manufactured goods of all kinds, attended by dealers and customers from a wide radius around. As social gatherings they also created a carnival atmosphere evident in the fun and carousing which accompanied the more serious business of buying and selling. Although Bath (the city proper) had long maintained two traditional fairs - the so-called 'cherry fair' on the feast of Saints Peter and Paul, granted in the fourteenth century, and the 'orange fair' dating from 1545, their *raison d'être* was already undermined well before 1700 by the rise of permanent markets and shops at the spa. In the eighteenth century they were each held for only one day, the cherry fair on 29 June (later 10

July), the other on 3 (later 14) February. Before 1800 they had shrunk to a line of temporary stalls in the Marketplace selling cheap fancy goods, millinery, and miscellaneous small wares. Any merrymaking must then have been confined to the nearby inns and taverns.

In comparison, the three-day 'Barton' fair on the flat top of Lansdown, a couple of miles out of Bath, retained more of the old character, for its open site was much better suited than the cramped town centre to receiving a large influx of countryfolk, farm animals, horses, cheeses, and other goods and produce, to say nothing of the sometimes boisterous entertainments. Details of these relate mainly to the later eighteenth century when the fair opened as always on 10 August, the feast of St Lawrence, and in fine weather drew a huge crowd onto the down, even at harvest-time, including many from Bath. Drinking booths were erected from boards, tressles and poles supplied by the nearby *Star* inn, but most diversions needed little equipment - 'bowling, fidling, raree shows, wild *beastesses*, with Punch and all his motley train' were prominent in 1793, besides many petty prizefight battles 'bravely, hardly fought'. Next year a report mentions the more ominous presence of EO tables, but also 'the usual display of conjurors, itinerant mummers, wild beasts, and gingerbread stalls'. In 1799 we hear of sleight-of-hand operators, singing girls, music grinders, tumblers, tall ladies, dancing bears, monkeys, and more bouts between pugilists from Bath and Bristol. On at least one occasion there was a roundabout.

Similar diversions, and similar excuses for hearty drinking, were found at various local revels, events which could easily degenerate into public disorder and which faced increasing judicial hostility in the last quarter of the century. Batheaston Revels were suppressed in 1775, the magistrates having had enough of fencers, showmen with bears, actors, minstrels, jugglers, petty chapmen, and confidence tricksters. Widcombe Revels came under a similar ban in 1787, this time imposed by the Bathforum magistrates, but neither the Bathforum nor the Bath bench could halt the Sabbath-breaking revelry, drinking and pugilism on Lansdown, which came under the Gloucestershire authorities. Though the Widcombe Revels were lost, the parish here kept its ancient Holloway Fair (originating like the Lansdown Fair in a grant of 1304) held every May. This too was popular enough to draw customers and sightseers out of Bath, and in 1754 added a horse fair to its attractions, 'there being great Encouragement for it given...'.

Fencing and Backsword

Wearing a small-sword to denote gentlemanly status declined in the early eighteenth century in favour of carrying a cane, so that basic skills in swordsmanship became even more confined to specialists and the military. The two distinct sciences of fencing and backsword were thus mainly spectator sports, except in the threatening 1790s when local militias were drilled in handling weapons. Fencing, with its strong overtones of gentility and duelling, employed a point weapon like a rapier or foil, which could be tipped with a button for safety in use. The common backsword, a single-edged cutting weapon, was potentially more dangerous in sporting combat, and for this reason a heavy stick with cane handle might sometimes be substituted for a sword proper. Less lethal, this could equally well 'break heads', in other words spill blood, the action which decided a bout. Backsword and its variant 'sword-and-dagger' came into the category of popular sports, for example being listed at the Coronation Day festivities at Bath in 1728 alongside boxing, wrestling and cudgelling. In 1735 a backsword match (the prize a laced hat) took place on Claverton Down during the races, but in 1737 Bath Marketplace was preferred for a gruelling 12-hour sword-and-dagger match in which each pair played six bouts. The Marketplace, just opposite the *White Lion*, was henceforth the site most often chosen for backsword contests, in spite of the impediment to traffic as crowds of onlookers wagered large sums on the outcome and the contestants, generally unpadded, battled gamely for a mere few guineas. Competitions lasting one or two days, sometimes in race week, were organised intermittently over the next few decades up to 1764, but by 1770 backsword seemed to be dying out - going the way of sword-and-dagger, wrestling, and quarter-staff, according to one regretful correspondent to the *Bath Journal*, who considered it a much worthier popular diversion than the common alternative of getting drunk.

Fencing and military swordsmanship came more to notice as backsword declined. In 1774 fencing was advertised for the first time as an educational extra at a Bath boys' school, the service perhaps provided by Boyle Arthur, a fencing- and dancing-master living in Stall Street. This was fencing regarded more as a polite accomplishment than a preparation for serious combat, but its practical usefulness became more evident from 1793 given the distinct risk of French invasion. In January 1794 Chabas junior, a Bristol fencing-master (perhaps an *émigré*), was already running a fencing school two days a week at Trim Bridge and

later helped train the Bath cavalry militia. From 1796 his successor, Thomas Galindo of the Bath Theatre Royal, taught the 'noble, manly, useful, and graceful Science' of the small-sword, as well as the cavalry technique of Hungarian broad-sword, first in Orange Court, then at the *Three Tuns* inn, and from January 1799 at the defunct Spring Gardens where he held public 'assaults' or displays of his pupils' elegant proficiency in 'Parades, Feints, and ornamental manoeuvres' of the small-sword. Interest in swordsmanship as an art had indeed been fanned in the winter of 1795-96 by a series of exhibition bouts performed by the famous transvestite but now elderly fencer, the Chevalière d'Eon, whose presence also attracted another great foreign master of the art, de Maison, to Bath. The more utilitarian handling of small-sword, Highland broadsword and sabre was otherwise covered from late 1799 by Galindo's Theatre colleague, John Edwin, at his Military Academy near St Michael's.

••• See also **Duelling**.

Festivities

Recurring festive events included the various fairs, the annual Mayor-making, the anniversaries of Charles II's Restoration on 29 May and, to a dwindling degree, the Gunpowder Plot on 5 November. Restoration or Oak Apple Day sometimes quite transformed the look of the city with symbolic foliage - notwithstanding the damage this was reportedly doing to all the oaks in the neighbourhood as late as 1799. Two generations earlier, on 29 May 1728, Bath had gone specially out of its way to impress the visiting Princess Amelia - the place resembled a green wood, ran one account, and people looked like walking boughs. Next day on the Princess's birthday the royalist Bath jeweller, Thomas Goulding, had morris-dancers perform outside her window in Westgate House, roasted a celebratory ox on nearby Kingsmead, and rounded off the evening with fireworks. This was his third homage to the dynasty in a row, the coronation in October 1727 and George II's birthday in November having already roused Goulding's instincts for spectacle: processions (with two companies of volunteer grenadiers), morris-dancing, country sports, oxen roasted in the Marketplace (one ox stuffed with jewels), hogsheads of beer, illuminations, bonfires, bells, and volleys of shot. Other individuals also took a lead - thus in 1758 Anne Pitt, sister of William Pitt (then war minister) got the Mayor's permission for a victory bonfire near the Circus at the news of the capture of Louisborough. For the most part, however, the joy at Hanoverian birthdays and war successes was orchestrated by the Guildhall, with the enthusiastic support of successive masters-of-ceremonies who organised grand balls and concerts to match. In 1738 the whole Corporation, alerted by Beau Nash to the Prince of Wales's approach, turned out to meet him at the city gate, the start of six weeks' jubilation that culminated with another civic procession to the Prince's lodging to acknowledge his favour to Bath. A stray comment made during this visit - 'we are an Epitome of London itself for Gaiety and Loyalty' - would be echoed at festivities down the century.

Royal appearances in wartime brought excitement to a feverish level: 'Grave as the times are', wrote Hannah More in January 1797, 'Bath never was so gay; princes and kings that will be, and princes and kings that have been, pop upon you at every corner...', meaning especially the princes of Wales and Orange on visits and the Yorks in almost permanent residence at this time in Royal Crescent. These produced the big occasions, the troop revues, the sumptuous dinners, the superb balls under the chandeliers. But there were many smaller jollifications of equal local significance, such as the laying of foundation stones and the optimistic toasts (with pails of strong beer for the workmen) that signalled the start of most large building projects, and the festivities at the completion of some of them - most famously the ridotto at the Upper Assembly Rooms in 1771. Some events went virtually unreported - the periodic beating of the city bounds, for example. Still others were private affairs - the merry rituals marking the completion of a 7-year craft apprenticeship, for example, or the mock funerals awarded by the sedan chairmen to any overindulgent colleague. By way of contrast, the spa occasionally fell into a sombre mood - on dates of national fasts (and packed churches) in the bleak war years, for example, or in July 1785 when retailers signalled their displeasure at Pitt's Shop Tax with black mourning cloths and weeping willows. But as a rule merriment far outweighed gloom and most people thought Bath a distinctly cheery place.

••• See also **Banquets; Bellringing; Fairs and Revels; Fireworks; Illuminations; Processions.**

Fireworks

Squibs, serpents and rockets were readily available. We hear of people letting them off in patriotic disdain for the Young Pretender in 1745-6, and at other times (including 5 November) throwing them dangerously about the streets, a practice the Corporation tried to stamp out in the 1780s. Properly staged displays were another matter, widely approved, often quite spectacular, and frequently linked to national celebrations and royal events. Rockets specially brought from the Tower of London for George II's coronation in 1728 proved rather a flop, but other celebratory displays went better (Queen Square 1739, and several held in the garden below North Parade 1746-9). In 1749 spectators flocked to Bath for the thanksgiving fireworks to mark the end of the long Austrian War - being promised 264 pumps, 200 sky rockets, Catherine wheels, air balloons, mines, fountains, and a set-piece pyramid topped by a sun. This gives some idea of pyrotechnic resources then possible. Almost every effect depended on mixtures of gunpowder, sometimes with iron filings and other ingredients added, to produce force, fire and sparks. What mattered more was the ingenuity of the fireworks engineer, especially in set-pieces like the illuminated Doric temple (fired by an artificial pigeon travelling fifty yards) seen at an extravaganza for the King's birthday in 1754. Most of these early displays seem to have been financed by subscription and sponsored by Nash, the master-of-ceremonies, but after his death the initiative passed to the pleasure gardens, starting with a brilliant show at Spring Gardens in July 1762.

It took the rivalries of pleasure gardens after 1785 to raise Bath fireworks into the top league however. Villa Gardens first threw down the gauntlet in 1786, and then a year later engaged Giovanni Invetto, a pyrotechnician from Milan, whose impact was felt at once, not just in the inventiveness of his Chinese fires, cascades, sparkling turning wheels, and balloons of stars and serpents, but in his exciting simulations of battle - the sieges of Gibraltar ('with the attack, defence, and destruction of the Floating Batteries') and of Portobelo. In 1788 Spring Gardens tried to meet Invetto's challenge by hiring the elder Clitherow from the London pleasure gardens. The rival programmes, full of novelties, were itemised in advertisements, some effects depending on Archimedes' screws, massed discharges of serpents and crackers, line rockets whizzing the length of the gardens, fanned Roman candles, and water fireworks.

Invetto's celebrity brought him commissions from Bristol, Devizes, Bradford and Frome, and the pressure on him perhaps bred carelessness. In August 1789 fireworks at his lodgings in Orange Court exploded, tragically killing his wife and son. Villa Gardens magnanimously allowed his benefit performance to be held at the more spacious Spring Gardens, which thereafter from 1790 to 1796 tended to monopolise his services. Nevertheless, Grosvenor Gardens called on Invetto in 1794, Sydney Gardens regularly from 1796, even St James's Palace garden on occasion, and Invetto organised his own benefit at Grosvenor in 1800. Fireworks were expensive but a sure draw at the handful of major evening galas held annually at the various garden venues. Invetto often prepared around fifteen principal pieces for each event - worth altogether more, he claimed, than any garden could actually pay, and 'universally allowed to be Master-Pieces of the Art' - among them his trademark battlepieces (e.g. the surrender of Valenciennes, shown 1793; Duncan's naval action against the Dutch, shown 1798) which had extra resonance in the war years from 1793 onwards. Records of personal reactions to fireworks at this period are very rare, but the King's birthday gala at Sydney Gardens in 1799 proves a notable exception, since at the repeat performance on 18 June Invetto made a palpable hit with Jane Austen. The illuminations were very pretty, she wrote later, but the fireworks had been really beautiful and surpassed all her expectations.

Florists' Feasts

Local gardening enthusiasts must have held feasts at Bath, as they did at Bristol and many other places, long before 1744 when they were first recorded. Essentially they were prize flower shows at which the competitors also dined sociably together. Horticulture was keenly practised at Bath, not just commercially but by many private gardeners and flower growers. Some of them specialised in particular plant families and genera. The report of a theft of 26 pots of ranunculus plants from a St Catherine's garden in 1744 scrupulously details the 21 different varieties taken, from 'Golden Chain' to 'Lady of Leghorn'. Ranunculus was a garden favourite, but in competitions auriculas and carnations reigned supreme. These were shown at separate annual shows in April and August respectively, often at the *George* in Walcot Street or the *Hand*

& *Flower* in Lansdown Road until about 1750 when the venue switched to Richard Lancashire's premises in Lyncombe. A society of 'gentlemen florists', i.e. non-commercial gardeners, must have set the competition rules and entry fees, appointed the judges, presented the prizes (e.g. silver spurs, a gold ring, a silver punch ladle) and ordered the dinner. By 1752 they were also running a subscription scheme for prosecuting garden thieves, and from 1763 to 1766 surely patronised the Theatre Royal whenever it put on the pantomime afterpiece, *The Auricula Feast, or Harlequin Florist*. Whether or not the award of the silver ladle in 1764 to a deceptively real-looking but artificial auricula, made by a Bath milliner, was a joke that misfired, it caused the florists' feast organisers some public embarrassment and gave rise to a sarcastic poem. However the competition went on until at least until 1770 and probably later, for the Gardeners' Society was still prosecuting its campaign against thieves and vandals into the 1780s.

••• See also **Botanic Gardens.**

Gambling

For perhaps 150 years, from the late Restoration period to the Regency, wealthy lovers of 'deep play' - both male and female - descended on Bath for the season, consorted with the professional experts in the gaming rooms, and gave the place something of a Las Vegas reputation.

Anecdotes of the great sums won and lost at Bath, and sometimes of the suicides and duels that ensued, circulated far beyond the spa, but these were only the dramatic peaks in a broader scene that included much gambling at a humbler level and across a far wider span of activities than just casino games. The magistrates bore down heavily from time to time. In 1713 they fined and later gaoled Thomas Sinnett for running a proscribed gaming house, and fined John and Philip Ditcher for a game of chance using illegally marked dice. In 1730 they suppressed another haunt 'where our servants lose their time, money, and honesty'. In 1731 they promised tough action against games like Faro. They spent a shilling on faggots to burn 'Little Dicks OE table' publicly in 1750, and seized similar equipment in 1781 and 1783. And they declared an intention to enforce the Act of 1765 against any journeymen, apprentices, servants, and labourers (together with the publicans involved) caught at any ale-house playing 'Cards, Dice, Draughts, Shuffle-Boards, Mississippi [a species of bagatelle], or Billiard-Tables, Skittles, Nine-Pins, or with any other Implement of Gambling'.

But gambling was endemic and the contagion strong. Any contest was good for a bet, from a whistling match (1711) or a walking race (1743) to the odds on a pair of sedan-chairmen being able to carry a heavy passenger $3^1/_2$ miles to Bathford non-stop (1761). Even quite ordinary citizens sometimes took shares in national lottery tickets or enjoyed a rubber of whist for a kitty of sixpences, half-crowns or even half-guineas. Grandees, for their part, would hazard fortunes. In September 1721 the Groom Porter (gambling officer to the Royal Household) returned to Bath for yet another season and soon the play was being called 'very deep'. It continued to be deep all through the 1720s. Wins and losses of several hundred pounds per session (to be multiplied by fifty or more for present-day equivalents) were almost routine. Baron Lechmere's wife lost 'such Furious summs... particularly £700 at one sitting' in 1725 that Lady Mary Wortley Montagu wondered 'whether all the sweetness that the Waters can put into my Lord's blood can make him endure it'. Next autumn a young beau was reported in tears after gambling away a few thousands. People became addicted to the flow of adrenalin. For the Earl of Chesterfield in 1737 it was almost a torture playing low 'which I hate, for the sake of avoiding deep play, which I love'. The 'Gamester Ladies' at Bath in 1714 used to hurry to the betting tables straight from morning service at the Abbey Church, and 'so highly reverence Play, as to make it a great part of their Exercise on *Sundays*'. Most clergy, while perhaps unwilling to profane the Sabbath, saw nothing wrong in a flutter themselves, so normal was the habit, so unobjectionable the ethos. A reference to Harrison's Assembly Rooms around 1727 described it, without irony, as 'a noble Room for Gaming' - gaming having become 'so much the Fashion amongst the *Beau-Monde*', according to another writer in 1734, 'that he who, in Company, should appear ignorant of the Games in Vogue, would be reckoned low-bred, and hardly fit for Conversation'.

Legislation in the years 1739-50 against certain card games, dice and forms of roulette had more visible effect than did increasing taxation on packs of cards (raised four times over the next half-century from 6d. to 2s.6d.) and pairs of dice. Now that there were legal limits on the sums which might be won or lost at a session, and within a space of 24 hours, Assembly Rooms gambling had abated from its former excesses. It was nonetheless far from given up - as might be guessed from the care the Upper Rooms took in stocking up before it opened in 1771 with an initial two gross of packs of cards for whist and another gross for piquet. Manuals on different games of chance were readily available, an early edition of Hoyle's famous treatise, with the calculation of probabilities, being issued at Bath in 1743. Other publications offered advice against fraudsters and all their 'operations, legerdemains, manoeuvres, artifices, tricks, shuffles, cuts, crosses...' as the *Annals of Gaming* advertised in 1775 - advice much needed at Bath where sharpers and confidence tricksters abounded. 'They infest the rooms, the promenades, nay... the very churches...', ran one warning in 1793, and indeed the last two decades of the century saw gambling, legal and otherwise, reach a new pitch. Twycross and Wetenall, notorious for their gaming house in Alfred Street, were convicted and fined in spring 1787, but their principal game, the illicit Faro, not only had aristocratic backing in London but powerful allies at Bath in the Duchess of Devonshire and Lady Duncannon. A Bath rout was said in 1791 to be hardly respectable without a Faro table, thus exposing the lame excuse for the formation of private card clubs that public card assemblies had been spoiled by the unwelcome presence of 'Greeks' or professional gamblers, 'Gentlemen who labour incessantly at their *Vocation of Betting*, and who... can calculate the chances to a Fraction...'.

The casino games highlighted in this section may have been the most prominent face of gambling at Bath, but betting underpinned plenty of other local pastimes, from racing and cockfights to billiards, bowling and bare-knuckle pugilism. Whatever form it took, the gambling industry was as much an element in local prosperity as the stone mines, the fashion trade, or the hot springs.

••• See also **Assemblies and Assembly Rooms** and under individual games and sports, e.g. **Cards**; **Dice**; **Horse-racing**.

Gardens see **Botanic Gardens**; **Pleasure Gardens**.

Guildhall

The Guildhall or Town Hall, symbol of Corporate identity and focus of local adminstration and justice, was transformed into a site of colourful bustle and jollification at times of civic festivities. It figured in the annual Mayor-making ceremony, hosted Corporation banquets, and was illuminated for the symbolic toasts to new monarchs or military and naval successes. The Stuart Guildhall, with the open market hall below and an early Georgian extension on its south side, contained a collection of Corporation and other portraits hanging round the main chamber. Like the Minerva head in a side room, these could readily be examined by interested visitors. The handsomeness of the Georgian Guildhall, which replaced its crumbling predecessor in 1777, must have impressed them still more. The lavish expenditure on this public building can be partly explained as a municipal rejoinder to the Upper Assembly Rooms from which civic dignatories were socially excluded. The assemblies here, under the city's own master-of-ceremonies, glittered especially brightly in the 1790s.

Horse and Carriage Sales

Horse fanciers had ample opportunity to indulge their passion at Bath. Riding, driving, equestrianism, racing, and eventually circus, were popular pursuits, backed up by every facility from livery stables, riding schools, farriers, and stud services to frequent sales of mounts and draught horses. Apart from the infrequent horse fairs, horses and teams were typically exhibited for sale at inns and stableyards. More systematic dealing dated from 1777. Regular Saturday sales were first tried at the Riding School and elsewhere, where connoisseurs of horseflesh could go to watch and buy. From 1786 Charles Demander ran the chief 'Horse Repository' or dealing centre, first at the *Pelican* in Walcot Street, and from 1794 in the yard of the disused *Bear* inn, while Jonathan Dash held

rival sales in the 1790s at the Riding School on Lansdown. Carriages were more often traded at the various city coachbuilders. Since a stylish equipage had high status-value, appraisal and trial of fashionable coaches, chariots, chaises, phaetons, gigs and whiskeys ranked seriously among the unsung pleasures of the spa.

Horse-racing

The early Bath race meetings had a chequered history, sometimes languishing for lack of support yet billed at other times (the 1770s in particular) as a premier event in the nation's sporting calendar. It was inevitable that racing - at first no doubt in the form of private challenge matches - would gravitate towards a spa where gambling was so closely woven into the culture. 'And hey for the Race on *Clarton*-Down', chirped *The Pleasures of the Bath* in 1721, still two years before the Corporation actually leased flat-topped Claverton from its landowner, William Skrine, to allow the visiting company to ride there. By 1728 Bath races had become an organised event, with a Town Plate to be run for on the usual system of three heats - and each heat of four miles with intervals for rubbing down between. Stamina as much as speed was needed for such gruelling performances, but the quality of bloodstock had been enormously improved over recent decades by selective breeding, and it became a common thing at Bath for a stud horse of good pedigree to be available at stated times to serve suitable mares. One 10-guinea purse run on the two-mile Claverton course in 1735 was in fact open only to the offspring of *Comely John*, a stallion owned by the landlord of the *Three Tuns*. But though Claverton staged at least three small race meetings that summer, so did many other West Country venues, diluting the quality of the field attracted to each event. The number of working days being lost nationally, not to speak of the ruinous betting, persuaded Parliament in 1740 to curb 'the Excessive Increase of Horse Races', and for a year or two Bath was subdued, the county gentry turning their attention to cock-fighting instead.

In February 1743 turfing appetites were whetted once more with a 10-mile contest between two local walkers lapping the race-track five times. Pedestrianism apparently broke the deadlock, for horse-racing recommenced that September with a two-day meeting. This was organised according to the unofficial 'Articles' that governed major meetings before the Jockey Club rules came in a decade later. No fewer than three reputable horses had to start, and those entered at the last minute ('at the post') paid double the normal $2^1/_2$-guinea entrance stake - with the runner-up receiving all the stake money and the winner the 50-guinea or £50 purse. The 1743 event failed to whip up much enthusiasm and racing lapsed again. Apart from the odd private match, and a parody contest in 1748 on Bath Common when crowds watched eleven boy jockeys ride asses for a guinea prize, racing at Claverton was not resumed until the two-day meetings staged in 1752 and 1756-58, which were accompanied by traditional backsword bouts and doubtless much sociability at the refreshment booths. Ralph Allen's purchase of Claverton manor in 1758 soon ended all that, even if he tolerated the fixture for one more year, 1759, in the knowledge that William Pitt, M.P. for Bath, had entered two runners. Except for a solitary trial event on Lansdown in 1765, more than a decade then elapsed before racing re-started on the old Claverton course with fresh vigour in September 1770. A grandstand with numbered seating was put up near the ancient Down House, together with a 'gallery' and on-site stabling to house an excellent field of thoroughbreds (including offspring of the celebrated champion *Eclipse*) for three days of racing for plate, cup or purse, with backsword contests and plenty of drinking on the side.

This was the start of a golden era. From 1771 the racing lasted a full four days. Proceedings were controlled by a steward and a clerk, with rules to cover everything from the jockeys' colours to the shooting of any dogs brought onto the course. By 1774 there was a Ladies' Purse of £50 and a Bath Cup of 100 guineas among the main races as well as sweepstakes and challenge matches. For the city it meant the fashionable autumn season opening earlier than usual, and a special zing in the air, full lodgings, 'ordinaries' (set-price meals) at the inns, nightly performances at the theatre, and balls at Gyde's and the new Upper Assembly Rooms. Nearly all the inns subscribed to the races and Gyde, significantly, was joint-owner of the Claverton grandstand. The zenith was attained in 1777 when as many as 800 carriages and 10,000 horse-riders and people on foot were estimated to have been on the down watching the sport. The Bath event remained a sporting highlight for several more years (as 'polite', stated the *Bath Guide*, as any next to Newmarket itself), but a decline was noticeable in 1782 when racing had to be abandoned on two of the four days for lack of runners. All the same, it was probably renewed hostility on the part of the current Claverton landowners that forced the organisers in 1784 into the 'long wished for' removal of the racecourse to the better turf of Lansdown. The site was also more convenient for Bristol and Gloucestershire racegoers, yet the field of runners that year was disappointing and racing ceased again until 1791.

The 1790s revival was spirited but lasted only a few seasons. Gradually the corded-off race track and other amenities on Lansdown were improved, a grandstand was erected, and again the 'après-race' social life enlivened the whole town. In 1793 large crowds watched the sport and the *Bath Chronicle* was even reminded of the best years on Claverton, except that the meeting was somewhat marred when part of the grandstand collapsed injuring a number of spectators. The following year the races were tried in May instead of the normal early autumn, but with less success, and in 1795, amid wartime crisis, high food prices and risk of popular disturbance, they were called off altogether. Resumed in October 1796, they were rather thinly attended despite expectations of royalty appearing. The Town Plate had to be abandoned altogether and the 120-guinea Bath Cup proved a disappointing walk-over. Times were clearly not propitious and again the Bath races lapsed, more seriously this time, and not in fact to be resurrected until 1811.

Illuminations

Eighteenth-century Bath might pride itself on its street-lighting, but even so the main thoroughfares were dim enough on moonless nights, and in certain parts of the city darkness reigned complete. Hence the feeling of magical transformation when whole streets and buildings were suddenly illuminated to celebrate some national occasion, or when pleasure gardens shone with ornamental lamps on gala nights. Hence too the popular

disapproval when prominent householders failed to do their bit, as for
instance at the proclamation of George II in 1727 when 'those that did
not illuminate felt the Resentment of the Mob by having their Windows
broke in pieces'. At this date it was mainly a question of placing sufficient
lighted wax candles in the windows (at Westgate House in 1727 'every
Window in a different manner'). The two Assembly Rooms and the
principal shops made Terrace Walk 'as light as noonday' in honour of
the Prince of Wales' marriage in 1736, and candles were out in force
again to accompany the bellringing, bonfires, and loyal toasts that saluted
victories and proclamations of peace in the 1740s and 1750s. Prior Park
was so bedecked in lights at the news of British success at Quebec in
1759, it conjured up, in one report, a chinoiserie vision of a feast of
lanterns.

   With the accession of George III in 1761, there is already evidence
of special devices being used to decorate public façades, and by February
1779 (during the rejoicings for Admiral Keppel's famous acquittal) the
sight of transparencies - semi-translucent pictures lit from behind - had
become almost commonplace. The pleasure gardens too seized on
transparencies to add extra glamour to their brilliant lamplit displays on
gala nights. Spring Gardens in 1786 and 1787 exhibited a particularly
fine array of transparencies after old master paintings, plus a further
example (hung in 1786 at the end of the 'lucid arched walk') of George
III in the guise of Henry V. The King's recovery of health merited a city
illumination in 1789, but Howe's 'Glorious First of June' in 1794 and
Nelson's Battle of the Nile in 1798 called forth quite unprecedented
displays of triumphal allegory onto the Bath streets, many of the
transparencies being carefully itemised in press accounts. Despite some
rain in 1798, the 'height, grandeur and uniformity of our buildings, rising
in many situations tier over tier, gave the illumination an affect and
advantages which no other place can boast of", crowed the *Bath Herald*.
Mrs Piozzi heard the reports and put it more tersely - 'This loyal City
shone away on the Rejoicing night I find...'.

Inns and Taverns

These were places of good cheer and sociability anyway, but sometimes
offered diversions besides. The chief coaching inns - *Angel, Bear,
Christopher, Lamb, Three Tuns, White Hart, White Lion*, and, from 1769,
the *York House* - presented endless human interest as people of all
conditions, high and low, locals and strangers, gravitated there or passed

through. Most of them had at least one large room available for meetings, parties, music, exhibitions, auctions, and like purposes. Some set space aside for billiards or, from the 1780s, to serve as a coffee-room with newspapers and comfortable chairs. A few inns and taverns were noted for particular activities, the *Lamb* in the 1730 and 1740s for its cockpit, the old *White Lion* for backsword contests (in the Marketplace outside), the *Globe* about 1747 for its short-lived theatre, the *Three Tuns* periodically for stallions at stud, the *Bear*, *Raven*, new *White Lion*, *White Hart* and (from 1803) *York House* all for catch clubs. In 1753 the gentry flocked to the *George* near the Cross Bath to witness the astonishing feats of a fire-eater, but almost as spectacular in its way was the annual Christmas treat furnished c.1760 by the *Jolly Butchers* in the Shambles - a 400-pound loaf more than 12 feet long and 2 broad, with a massive cheese or two to match. Horses, carriages and wagons were often auctioned from inn stableyards, which also served on occasion for shows of exotic beasts. A house like the *Queen's Head* in Cheap Street played host to book auctions, exhibitions, and public lectures, and around 1780 contained a 'Lilliputian Theatre' where such shows as the *ombres chinoises* or the *fantoccini* marionettes appeared. The *Saddlers Arms*, close by at the top of Stall Street, meanwhile provided an upstairs room for auctions and exhibitions, and round the corner in Westgate Street the *Angel* at different times exhibited religious sculpture, a prize ox, and an Irish giant.

Lectures and Readings

The medium of the public lecture was still a novelty in 1724 when J.T.Desaguliers, a pioneering London expositor of science, held forth at Bath about a current eclipse of the sun. Within the next fourteen years Desaguliers returned at least four more times to deliver popular courses on astronomy and physics (optics, mechanics, hydrostatics, etc.), always explaining the theory alongside practical applications, and demonstrating with the help of measuring devices, optical instruments, prisms, levers, model engines, pumps, and a small planetarium, all brought with him from the capital. Henceforth, science lecture courses with experiments enacted directly in front of an audience became a winning formula. Entertainment blended with instruction, science became fashionable, and a string of visiting and local lecturers kept Bath audiences abreast of discoveries and inventions all through the century. One central figure, the instrument-maker Benjamin Martin, who lived at Bath in the later

1740s, lectured to spa audiences and also experimented with the electrical phenomena recently made so accessible and popular through the invention of the Leyden jar. (A showman at the *Queen's Head* in 1746 promised his customers truly shocking sensations - 'the Electrical Commotions to be felt by every Person in the Room, and the Fire to come out of any Part of the Body'.)

In the second half of the century itinerant lecturers such as Ferguson, Griffiss, Warltire, Lloyd, Walker jun., and the blind Moyes, regularly gave series of 6, 10, 12 or even more subscription lectures, as did the resident lecturer John Arden and Benjamin Donn(e) of Bristol. A scientific colleague of Joseph Priestley, Warltire outlined their ground-breaking research on the chemistry of gases. Courses on astronomy featured elaborate orreries for illustrating the movement of heavenly bodies (Lloyd's transparent orrery measured 21 feet across), sometimes in a succession of theatrical 'scenes' accompanied by music to rouse feelings of religious awe. Not all topics were quite so uncontroversial - Mesmerism, for instance, in 1791 - and during the politically tense 1790s most lecturers tended to play safe anyway by concentrating, if not on astronomy, then on subjects such as natural history, healthy diet, and even the veterinary science of the horse's foot.

With their surprising experiments and seeming command of natural phenomena, the science lecturers had a whiff of the magician about them and could easily make good their claim to provide 'rational amusement' for both sexes. It was harder work for lecturers on other topics. The artist Thomas Malton jun. had only a small audience for his course on perspective (with equipment of some kind) in 1777, though Christopher Pack did better in 1797, speaking on the theory and practice of fine art. In 1763, and again in 1770-1, Thomas Sheridan, the playwright's father, was probably the first at Bath to try what he called lectures on 'oratory' but which essentially comprised dramatic readings from literary classics. (Samuel Johnson told his biographer Boswell that he feared Sheridan's attempt was undermined in advance by the mockery Bath's master-of-ceremonies Derrick had poured on it.) Sheridan's followers in this genre included the Bath man-of-letters-cum-bookseller S.J.Pratt (alias Courtney Melmoth), whose readings at the Assembly Rooms in 1783 were said to be 'very brilliantly attended', and also Henry Brown, formerly with the Orchard Street theatre, who performed in 1785, as Pratt himself did a second time. The most entertaining shows of this sort, however, were the one-man renderings of complete French plays, in the original, by the

well-known Antoine Le Texier who visited Bath regularly c.1786-99 to
much acclaim from audiences able to follow the language. The 'hearty
laugh' Henry LeFanu enjoyed at two of Le Texier's mornings in 1790
must have done him more good, his wife thought, than all the spa water
he'd so far drunk for his health.

Menageries

Wild-beast shows touring from London now and then gave Bathonians
an opportunity to thrill at the sight of exotic creatures known otherwise
only from picture books and travellers' tales, some of them rarities newly
imported and hardly yet studied or classified. The eleven mammals
shown alongside a golden eagle and two 'Sepulchre' vultures at the
Wheatsheaf in 1755 included hyenas, a chimpanzee, mandrill, marmoset,
jackal and porcupine. In 1757 the first crocodile arrived, and in 1763,
accompanied by a dromedary and probably two species of leopard, came
a 'most astonishing SEA-MONSTER', in reality a young sea lion
captured off the Siberian coast. Not every creature can be identified with
certainty from contemporary descriptions, but among the novelties over
the next few years were tigers, a baboon, a 'Flying Dragon', a likely
python, various South American fauna (monkeys, armadillo, alpaca,
brightly coloured macaws), and the first (much-admired) zebra to be
shown publicly in Britain. Most often the animals were exhibited at local
inns, sometimes in the stuffy wagons they were conveyed in, sometimes
outside in cages and pens or kept chained up. An American visiting Bath
witnessed a mandrill at the *Cross Keys* in 1780 and copied down much
of the showman's advertisement in his diary, including a section about
the ape sitting in a chair holding a club and drinking from a bottle. Another
mandrill appeared in a typically mixed collection in 1784 with a lion,
cheetah, black wolf, and various monkeys - 'All well secured, and kept
clean'.

The travelling shows of the 1790s largely drew on the zoo at London's
Exeter 'Change known variously as Pidcock's, Polito's, and Cross's.
Pidcock brought two dozen or more specimens in 1791, first to Lansdown
Fair, then to a field at Bathwick. Besides a tiger, lioness, hyena, 'African
Ram' (a breed of fat-tailed sheep) and two ostriches, he paraded freaks
of nature like a two-headed heifer and a three-legged colt. In 1794 his
solitary exhibit was spectacular enough, 'a most Wonderful Living Male
ELEPHANT' just landed from India, the first in Britain for over twenty
years, which he kept in a caravan in Beaufort Square and fulsomely

advertised for its amazing sagacity, strength, bulk and gentleness, not forgetting either its valuable tusks and peculiar trunk 'which is a long cartilaginous tube hanging between its teeth, wherewith it feeds itself'. Three more Indian elephants, each in its own caravan, excited Bath in 1797, backed up by an 'Indian Antelope' (perhaps a blackbuck) and a male nilghai, an even larger Indian ruminant. Cross's menagerie in 1799 once again featured a 'stupendous' elephant, plus hyena, 'Arabian Savage' (Hamadryas baboon?) and a Hudson Bay horned owl. This time, though, the big cats took pride of place with tiger, cheetah, 'ring-tailed' leopard, and pairs of both lions and pumas. And late in 1800, Polito's caravans en route for Bristol Fair gave Bath a chance to see yet more exotics - storks, a genet, a Barbary ape, a kangaroo, and an unnamed beast from Bengal that still awaited scientific description - all of which 'the most timorous may approach with the greatest safety'.

Music see **Catch Clubs**; **Church- and Chapel-going**; **Concerts**; **Pump Room**; **Theatre**; **Waits Music**.

Natural History see **Menageries**; **Science and Natural History**.

Pastrycooks' Shops

The eighteenth-century pastrycooks' shops resembled delicatessens and take-aways, except that some would also lend the use of their ovens to cook customers' dishes prepared at home. Bath had plenty of such establishments, but only two merit inclusion here for their place on many visitors' schedules, Gill's and Molland's. While doing the rounds of the shops 'we... commonly stop at Mr. Gill's, the pastry-cook, to take a jelly, a tart, or a small bason of vermicelli', Lydia remarks in Smollett's *Humphry Clinker*, closely echoing Christopher Anstey in his versified

New Bath Guide: 'If the weather, cold and chill, / Calls us all to Mr. Gill, / Romeo hands to me the jelly, / Or the soup of vermicelli...'. Anstey indeed printed a whole ditty of fourteen verses extolling Charles Gill's ambrosial soups, spit-turned chickens, savoury grills, and other gourmet delights, which included sweet as well as savoury items to eat on the spot or carry out. The shop stood from 1756 at the sign of the Pheasant in Wade's Passage, crammed up against the north flank of the Abbey Church, its chimney protruding beside a buttress, its mouth-watering display window fronting the busy pedestrian passage between Abbey Churchyard and Orange Grove. In the 1780s, after Gill's death, the business was run by others, but by then Nicholas Peter Molland, a French cook from Brighton, had seized the initiative. After two years in Northgate Street he moved in late 1781 to upmarket Milsom Street, no.2 at the sign of the Cock, a prime location on the west side facing the Octagon chapel. The premises were more spacious than Gill's and contained a proper dining room where the politician John Wilkes twice gourmandised in January 1783 with parties that included the current master-of-ceremonies at the Lower Rooms. This or another room was large enough to be hired for private dances and suppers, as we know from a party enjoyed by c.15 young couples early in 1793 and mentioned in a letter by one satisfied participant, Elizabeth Canning. Molland's 'temple' ('Immortal Molland! as immortal as Gill') likewise attracted notice in fiction and verse, most famously in *Persuasion* when Miss Elliot shelters there from a shower of rain - quite conceivably as Jane Austen herself did on occasion. But in another account, Molland's, good though it was admitted to be, seemed 'deadly dear'.

Pleasure Gardens

Picture them as semi-rural versions of the Assembly Rooms, providing outdoor venues for the polite world to meet, stroll, take refreshments, sometimes to dance or hear music (and possibly to gamble at cards and dice, though no evidence has yet been forthcoming), all in a setting of trees and lawns, parterres and birdsong. In the warmer months these green enclosures became a chief attraction, select but sociable, ideal for breakfastings and tea parties as well as for fashionable evening galas with lamplit walks, scurrying waiters, full-scale concerts, and spectacular fireworks. Unlike Bath's various promenades and riverside paths which were public places and open to everyone, the pleasure gardens offered reasonable privacy and a degree of social exclusiveness, largely maintained by charging for admission and insistence on proper dress. Following Vauxhall and Ranelagh in London, they evolved in time from simple green retreats to private suburban parks planned with special features - arbours, bandstands, bowling greens, swings, mazes and grottoes - though the smaller out-of-town gardens did retain an air of country simplicity.

Harrison's Walks, which began the sequence at Bath, was unusual in being a physical appendage to the Assembly Rooms. Laid out below the city walls around 1709, when Harrison's Rooms opened on Terrace Walk, it was reached by stairs at the rear of the premises. Allées of lime trees and an espaliered path by the Avon made it agreeably bucolic in the late spring and summer (Bath's visiting season up to nearly 1730). A brick summerhouse with long rusticated windows overlooked the river in one corner. This contained a statue of an 'enthroned deity' and no doubt served as an extra refreshment room. A much-faded fan drawing of 1737 depicts this building with fashionable company strolling nearby and a pleasure boat on the river. In the early 1740s the massive construction of North Parade destroyed the garden's privacy but provided a fine viewpoint over the bowling green and for special events like the celebratory fireworks staged in 1749 and later. The twenty cannon that Nash obtained from Bristol in 1745 were long kept here ready to be fired off on big occasions, and the garden remained open for walking, bowling, and occasional breakfast concerts despite the rubbish tipping from North Parade on its south side.

Some years before the Parades were built, Spring Gardens had already begun its lengthy career, just a ferry boat ride away across the river. Here an enclosed plot was originally leased in 1737 to William Hull, a gardener, who failed to exploit its potential and who had such arrears of rent by 1742 that his landlord, William Pulteney (1st Earl of Bath), replaced him with a new tenant, Edmondson, and erected a better garden house. During Edmondson's 17-year tenure the attractions included a bowling green, *al fresco* country dancing, and good victualling, but more effective promotion had to wait until William Purdie took over in April 1759. Purdie, a manservant made good, was a wine-merchant and lodgings-keeper in Orange Court who acted as Pulteney's rent collector in Bathwick and held half rights in the ferryboat sevice - which he now shifted fifty yards downstream directly opposite the gardens. Through the 1760-70s he established a summer routine of public and private breakfastings, occasional public teas, and evening entertainments with music, dancing and fireworks. His clients subscribed 2s.6d.for the season or paid 6d. a time for a brass entrance disc which entitled them to a hot drink, wine or a jelly at the bar. Hot breakfast rolls and Sally Lunns (probably invented here) were specialities, and as usual with pleasure gardens it was catering that must have produced the chief profits. Spring Gardens under Purdie grew more sophisticated: flowerbeds, classical urns, a water canal and cascade lined the avenues; clarinets and horns played for cotillions and country dancing; and a full orchestra (led by William Herschel among others) sometimes performed quite enterprising programmes. Easily accessible by ferry, and from 1774 across Pulteney Bridge, it was patronised well enough not to be troubled in 1770 by the rise of a modest new pleasure garden, half-a-mile out of Bath at the corner of Allen's Drive and Lyncombe Vale.

This, the Bagatelle, was associated with a recently discovered medicinal spring and the long-established attraction of Wicksteed's Machine, a seal-engraving mill. By summer 1772, under James Wicksteed and his caterer Mrs Bowers, the garden was promoting musical breakfastings and dancing twice a week, plus evening entertainments that included a lamplit waterfall and doubtless made use of the 'canal' that supplied the existing millwheel. When Wicksteed departed in 1774, James Guillet, a carver-and-gilder, succeeded him and added a new feature, a narrow 60-yard-long men's bathing pool in an orchard behind the main site. Guillet left in 1776/77 after complaining of enemies to the enterprise, to be followed by T.Harrison of London who briefly re-opened in 1778 but then gave up altogether. One reason may have been the launch in 1777 of a rival garden under the name of King James's Palace, prettily contrived on a narrow sloping site higher up Lyncombe Vale facing the former Lyncombe Spa. Initially this garden had freemasonic connections through its proprietor, Charles Waters, a master tailor of Bath with a taste for fossil-collecting. He or his son Harry, who briefly ran the garden before a tenant took the lease, made a feature of the green- and hot-houses, frequently advertising the sale of plants alongside the more obvious notices of breakfastings, dinners, and twice-weekly evening band performances. The tranquillity and beauty of the setting were nevertheless perhaps the greatest draw, as certain escapist verses printed in *Bath Journal* 18 Sep 1780 (just after the Gordon Riots had troubled Bath) clearly suggest. After Waters sold up in 1789, King James's Palace was briefly run by a former waiter from the *Bear* inn, Robert Lansdown, and then from 1791 by a perfumer, Robert Tanner, who after another two years and five spirited experiments with evening galas (fireworks and all) finally closed the now bankrupt enterprise during the national financial crisis of 1793.

Spring Gardens meanwhile faced a tougher opponent in Bathwick Villa Gardens, which occupied a site near the present Henrietta Gardens. Fanny Burney has left a comic account of the indoor entertainment presented here in 1780 by the retired silk merchant James Ferry, but it was a local wine retailer, Joseph Marrett, who from 1783 onwards turned this small estate and 'Gothick'-style house into an orthodox pleasure garden with the usual breakfastings and afternoon teas accompanied by serenading musicians. It soon emerged as a formidable, albeit smaller, rival to Spring Gardens, claiming that its location was drier and healthier. Its bandstand was apparently large enough to hold the 23 musicians who played at a gala in 1786, and Marrett set standards in displays of coloured lanterns and transparencies and fireworks that Spring Gardens was obliged to match. Both gardens engaged in strenuous competition in the later 1780s, most notably at their evening fêtes to mark royal anniversaries, when neither proprietor stinted on novelties or catering, and Spring Gardens sometimes sold more than 2000 entrance tickets. The rising number of gentry settling permanently at Bath helps explain why pleasure gardens could attract such good custom in the summer months, usually the slack season for visitors.

However well they fared, though, both attractions were now under threat from Pulteney's vast building project for Bathwick. In 1790 Marrett held only one grand entertainment at Bathwick Villa, and this was his last public gesture before he sold off to James Cross of the Bath City Bank, an institution concerned in the financing of new Bathwick and with no interest in preserving a public garden. Spring Gardens (or Vauxhall as it was now dubbed) still survived on borrowed time. The widowed Mrs Purdie, lessee since 1783, handed over in 1790 to her son-in-law, Meshach Pritchard, manager of the Parade Coffee House, who energetically continued her policies until June 1795. Although the arrival of two major new pleasure gardens in the 1790s would fatally undermine the institution, it went out defiantly with a run of often crowded gala occasions always enlivened by concerts and brilliant fireworks. Its final tenant, John Townsend, was nonetheless forced to appeal in August 1795 to a more workaday clientèle than formerly by starting a tradesmen's coffee room. Three years later, after one last grand gala and some sixty years' activity, the grounds closed for good.

B A T H

Spring-Gardens, Vauxhall.

ON TUESDAY next June 17, and every Tuesday during the season as usual, will be a CONCERT of Vocal and Inftrumental MUSIC, with ILLUMINATIONS, after the manner of Vauxhall, London.

Principal Vocal Performers; Mrs.Warrel, Mr.Waterhoufe, Mr. Howell, Mr. Ruffell, Mafters Gray and Sheppard, &c.

Firft Violin Mr. Brooks, Oboe Mr. Afhley, and Violoncello Mr. Herfchell.——To begin at Seven o'clock.

CATCHES and GLEES each night.

With a grand Difplay of FIRE-WORKS,

By the firft Artift in London, engineer to Ranelagh and Marybone Gardens, who has had the honour of exhibiting feveral pieces of Fire-Works before his prefent Majefty and the reft of the Royal Family at Kew; likewife at Gunnerfbury and Ranelagh Gardens, for the entertainment of his Danifh Majefty.

Tickets 1s. each, to be had at the Gate of the Gardens. And on THURSDAY next (and every Thurfday 'till the Theatre finally clofes, after which it will be changed to Saturdays) will be a PUBLIC TEA, attended with French-horns, Clarionets, &c. Tickets 1s. each, which entitle the bearer to Tea or Coffee.

N. B. The road will be properly watered every publick night.

In its closing years Spring Gardens had links with Grosvenor Gardens, one of its successors. In fact before taking on Spring Gardens Townsend had helped to finance and manage the Grosvenor development. Furthermore the Grosvenor's architect, John Eveleigh, held a stake in Spring Gardens through his wife, another Purdie. By contrast, the second project of the 1790s, Sydney Gardens, realised under the Pulteney aegis, had no connection with any other, even if it did usurp Spring Gardens' title of Vauxhall. Plans for both ventures, on a larger scale than their predecessors, were announced in summer 1791, but Grosvenor, well out on the London road, got off to a quicker start. It was receiving company for tea and wine in September 1792, and within another year boasted two bowling greens, an archery field, maze, Merlin's swings, fishponds, and pleasure boats on the Avon which bounded it on the south. Eveleigh the architect, Richard Hewlett the builder, William and John Townsend, silversmiths, and two Bath banks had financed the speculation, mostly on mortgage, but after the crash of 1793 a shareholders' trust was created to rescue the scheme.

Sydney Gardens, on the other hand, was managed by an investment trust from the start, and from 1794 Charles Harcourt Masters shouldered responsibility for the design of both garden and an intended hotel. The garden opened in very rudimentary form in spring 1795 under John Gale, a hosier and haberdasher by trade. During his time of management (until

1799, and again from 1801, with T.Holloway intervening) he steadily eroded the Grosvenor's lead, successively introducing bar facilities, bowling, grotto, maze (with a Merlin's swing for healthy exercise), winter opening, a perimeter horse ride, refreshment boxes, a cold bath, and other features. By summer 1796 he was able to announce his first gala, two years after the Grosvenor, with romantic illuminated walks, a vocal and instrumental concert, and lavish pyrotechnics. The crush of 4000 who attended the gala was unprecedented and in future tickets went on sale in advance. In July 1796 the Prince of Wales patronised Sydney Gardens in person, assuring its fashionability, and the hotel necessary to complete the whole scheme was begun soon after and ultimately realised, with coffee-, card- and billiard-rooms and semi-circular bandstand at the rear, in 1799. By that date the Avon & Kennet canal was beginning to slice through the site, but far from spoiling the garden only came to improve its appeal to contemporaries, along with the canopied bowers, pavilions, thatched umbrellas, waterfalls, and sham castle that were also added about this time. Grosvenor Gardens, in comparison, had ceased to innovate. Run by William Hewlett 1795-7 and then E.Davis, it too had an associated hotel, but was always more rural in feel than its rival, a place to row a boat or listen to nightingales. While it was still capable of staging occasional concerts and fireworks the equal of those at Sydney Gardens, its distance from central Bath left it at a disadvantage in terms of regular custom and hence of sufficient income. As the century closed, Grosvenor's days were beginning to look numbered.

    ••• See also **Breakfasting; Concerts; Fireworks; Illumina-tions; Wicksteed's Machine.**

Poetry Contests

'... a very diminutive property with large pretensions' was Horace Walpole's prescient verdict in 1766 on the Batheaston villa at which he had just dined with Capt. John Miller and his wife. A few years on, the Millers returned from their Grand Tour with some awareness of Italian literary academies and a tangible souvenir in the shape of a large Roman vase purchased at Frascati. Around these two poles Mrs (later Lady) Miller fashioned the rites of the Batheaston Vase, fortnightly morning *assemblées* for the great and the good and the literary, who drove out to the villa from Bath for elegant refreshments and, the high spot of the visit, the crowning of the victorious poets. Some suitable theme, or in the early days a set of rhymed line-endings, was prescribed in advance of the gathering so that would-be versifiers might compose in whatever leisure they could spare 'amidst the hurry of plays, balls, public breakfasts, and concerts, and all the dissipations of a full *Bath Season*... alike unfriendly to Contemplation and the Muses' (to quote Anna Miller herself). At the subsequent ceremony their offerings were cast into the ribboned vase, withdrawn in turn, read aloud, and finally judged, and the first, second and third then received their bouquet, wreath or myrtle sprig. The 'instituters of the poetical prizes', it was observed, were assiduous in courting people of rank. Dozens of coaches stood parked near the villa on vase mornings. It was the *ton* to be there, acknowledged the *Bath Chronicle* in January 1781 as it listed some of the nobility present. In Edmund Rack's more jaundiced view the year before it was 'all parade & ceremony & Chocolate & Jellies & Creams which by repetition lose their power of pleasing', yet it was a ceremony with staying power, surviving nine years until its hostess's sudden death in 1781. Nationally its fame was spread by published selections of the prize-winning verses. Four successive volumes of *Poetical Amusements of a Villa near Bath* appeared from 1775 to 1781, the profits earmarked for a charitable cause. Affected, snobbish and somewhat ludicrous, a coterie such as this laid itself open to the satire it duly received. That it nevertheless shrugged off all efforts at ridicule, and furthermore mustered defenders (Christopher Anstey included), showed a stubborn refusal on its adherents' part to have their enjoyment curtailed by spoilsports of any sort.

Popular Sports

Just before the old bowling green behind Terrace Walk was redeveloped in the late 1720s, John Wood relates that people used it for 'Smock Racing and Pig Racing, playing at Foot-Ball and running with the Feet in Bags... and Jig[g]ing upon the Stage for Rings, Shirts, Smocks, Hats, &c.' Other open spaces in and about Bath must have served similar purposes at different times, for children as well as adults, though seldom recorded in print except for a passing mention of 'chuck' (probably chuckie-stones, i.e. pitch-and-toss) in 1751. A number of everyday pastimes were considered good exercise: in his *Essay of Health and Long Life* Dr Cheyne thought even football had its value. The authorities frowned on the rowdier activities and attempted to stamp out any that, as time passed, came to offend eighteenth-century sensibilities. The best example here is the old Shrovetime custom of Throwing at Cocks, i.e. aiming missiles at specially purchased cockerels imprisoned in pots, which the byelaws prohibited from c.1756 onwards as a barbarous activity. The Bath Improvement Act of 1793 also contained a clause to stop football, fives and other annoying games being played in the streeet.

••• See also **Boxing; Cockfighting; Fencing and Backsword; Shooting; Skittles.**

Processions

Street processions were passing entertainments anyone could watch. Some positively demanded attention - the performers and drummer parading about town to advertise a show, for instance. Even a funeral had a brave appearance if it employed the full panoply of the 'Black Work' - black hearse, four black coaches, black chariot, and teams of plumed black horses. Beau Nash was thus interred at the Abbey Church in February 1761after a splendidly impressive cortège: a choir of Charity School children singing a solemn hymn at the front, followed by the Pump Room band and the City Waits playing alternately with the choir, then three clergymen with the draped coffin supported by six aldermen, and behind these the two Assembly Rooms proprietors as chief mourners, and finally other Corporation members and gentry, all of it done to the tolling of muffled bells and punctuated by gun salutes at one-minute intervals.

The Mayor and aldermen (in scarlet finery) and city councillors were used to processing on other civic occasions and did it grandly from the Guildhall to the Abbey Church and back every October at the start of the mayoral year. Sometimes they marked other dates and events with street pomp. In 1752 they deliberately chose a regular Bath festival, the commemoration of the Stuart Restoration, on which to give official blessing to the reborn city companies (or freemen's guilds). The seven reinstituted companies with painted insignia marched from Walcot Street to the Guildhall to join the waiting Shoemakers' and Taylors' companies who, with musicians, Mayor's officers, and Mayor and Corporation, then filed to the Abbey Church for a service and sermon, and afterwards to Broad Street for the laying of the first stone of the new Grammar School - the streets crowded throughout with spectators and 'what added a double Lustre to the Whole, was the brilliant Appearance of LADIES, who beheld the Sight from the Balconies and Windows'. Two years later, with a large muster of clergy and gentry, they once more processed to the School, now fully built, for the inaugural speech of the Headmaster. In 1760 the

Corporation, the beflagged companies, music, clergy and gentry paraded yet again as the Town Clerk proclaimed George III's acccession at six different points of the city to cheering throngs and pealing bells.

Public philanthropy gave rise to more sentimental, condescending kinds of spectacle. John Penrose watched on Charity Sunday 1766 as hospital patients were twice lined up in the nave of the Abbey Church to allow the Corporation procession and congregation to pass between the rows: and 'when they went from Church, they all walked two and two very orderly, four Beadles with staves preceding, then the Men Patients, then two more Beadles, then the Women Patients, then the other two Beadles closing the Processsion'. The crocodiles of Sunday School children wending their way to church in the late 1780s rather similarly expressed community good works, just as in the nineties the sight of the various benefit societies marching proudly with their emblematic flags, ribbons and white wands proclaimed the message of self-help. Military processions on the other hand spelt patriotism and reassurance. Examples here are all the parading and public drilling of Ralph Allen's troop in their blue and red uniforms at the time of the Jacobite scare in 1745-6, or the ceremonious presentation of colours to the Bath militia cavalry and infantry at Sydney Gardens in June 1799.

Promenading

Not unlike a *passeggiata* in function, promenading at Georgian Bath might be defined as making a conspicuous appearance at set times on the public walks - or, in bad weather, strolling about the Assembly Rooms (and in pre-Assembly Rooms times in the Abbey Church) - with the primary objective of seeing and being seen. By the very fact of promenading one really staked a claim to inclusion within the charmed circle of the upper crust. It was an opportunity for self-display, if possible with a supporting cast of family and friends. Other pleasures and benefits of the promenade - the pleasant settings, the fresh air and gentle exercise, the happy encounters and useful introductions, the chance to gossip - were fortuitous by-products. The public stage was the thing, and the costume and the acting had to be appropriate. During the parading hours (originally from about noon to two, but eventually rather later as the hour of dinner slipped; after church on Sundays; in the earlier decades on summer evenings too) the dress, demeanour and sheer numbers of the participants must have served to warn off undesirable intruders.

Before 1700 the favoured promenades were, as Celia Fiennes reported, the tree-lined walks immediately east and south of the Abbey Church, and other paths in Kingsmead meadows where small cake-houses sold syllabubs and drinks. After 1700 the further evolution of Gravel Walks and Terrace Walk brought the area behind the Abbey Church, with its luxury shops, coffee-house and Assembly Rooms, even more into vogue - 'thronged every Evening with the most agreeable of both Sexes'. The creation in the early 1720s of Wade's Passage, a pedestrian thoroughfare from Gravel Walks to the Abbey Churchyard, and then twenty years later the construction of the Parades overlooking the river, resulted in a fine pennant-sandstone pavement, several hundred yards long, from the Pump Room all the way to South Parade and so smooth that it was 'as easy walking there, as in a floored Room'. From the 1740s onwards this whole length was virtually a promenade, though the company now gravitated to one particular part of it, the Parades, especially Grand (i.e.North) Parade which offered a traffic-free backwater with perspectives of green hills.

According to one visitor, as late as 1777 the Parades remained the most frequented promenade, only he added that in colder weather the company tended to resort to the Crescent. In fact the huge expansion of the upper town had already made Crescent Fields the modish new stamping ground. The site was altogether more private than the Parades, and it was no wonder that in 1773 the landowner Earl Rivers' proposal to turn this pasture into market gardens caused outrage and never went further. As the socialite Elizabeth Montagu enthused in 1780, below the Crescent itself and commanding a splendid country view lay 'a beautiful green lawn fenced by an Iron rail, where sheep are feeding, and to this enclosure the Inhabitants of the Crescent have a key, so that it serves as a general garden for walking'. Elizabeth Sheridan wrote in similar delighted terms in 1786. She called it 'the present Mall of Bath' and felt 'something whimsical yet pleasing in seeing a number of well-dress'd people' strolling among grazing cattle and horses. Access to Crescent Fields from Queen Square and the town side was further improved in 1789 after Gravel Walk, by then almost impassable, was reinstated by public subscription. Closer to the centre, Milsom Street grew increasingly popular as the place to go in the decades around 1800 - and not for the smart shops alone. Several accounts hint of the obsessive strolling here, and of much walking up Milsom Street simply in order to walk down again.

••• See also **Rambling**.

Pump Room

The rather elegant orangery-style Pump Room erected against the King's Bath in 1706 provided a much-needed sheltered space in which invalids could take their prescribed glasses. It had an equally valuable second role. From about seven in the morning, and especially between eight and ten, it served as a meeting place for genteel company - patients and non-patients alike - in the hours before the Assembly Rooms opened. It had no special rules. People might attend without ceremony in 'undress' (i.e. informal attire) and socialise noisily amid all the popping of pills and quaffing of mineral water. The Pump Room was one of the few civic amenities which the Corporation itself provided for visitors, but this was done at arm's length by renting out both Pump Room and baths to an official manager, the Pumper, who usually held it for profit over two years. The Pump Room musicians, on the other hand, came under the wing of the master-of-ceremonies. Normally paid for out of the same subscription as the balls, this band of six to ten performers supplied a cheerful programme of string and wind pieces every weekday in the season as long as the fund lasted - or attempted to supply because, as John Penrose observed, it was hard to hear their pleasant 'Tweedle-dum and Tweedle-dee' above the hubbub. From 1771 onwards the squabbles for market share between the two Assembly Rooms began to affect the sums available for the Pump Room music. A special subscribers' committee never really resolved this awkward issue which was felt to affect even city centre traders, since the music drew 'the visitor and inhabitant from the most distant parts of the city to one general place of morning rendezvous... [where] the inspiring melody of the Orchestra spreads a general glow of happiness around...'.

This quotation dates from 1799, less than four years after the Pump Room had been re-opened following a complete rebuild on the optimistic scale befitting the boom years around 1790. The earlier building had been remodelled in 1732-34 and extended 1751-2, but had never kept up with the seasonal crush of visitors (illustrated by Mrs Delany's comment on one occasion - 'attempted the pump-room - *so crowded no admittance*'). Sited for so long at the heart of visitors' Bath, it was a veritable fount of news and gossip. It held the 'book of intelligence' in which new arrivals inscribed their names (a main source for the newspaper columns), posted on its walls official information (such as the list of sedan chairmen and fares), and sometimes hung exhibitions to publicise artists then in town. A young visitor in 1788 found it magnetic

- the flowers by the entrance, the silver balls (to distract flies), Nash's full-length statue, the rising columns of steam, the musicians, and 'the vast ever-shifting throng of gaily dressed company'. Being able to stare out of its windows onto the bubbling bath and the bathers below always surprised newcomers to the spa. Earlier in the century, spying on the bathers had offered even better sport at the fashionable Cross Bath, which was then equipped with a musicians' gallery to entertain spectators and health-seekers alike.

Puppet Shows

The fact that in the earlier eighteenth century puppet shows could be described on their London visits and provincial tours as 'Powell's puppet-show from the Bath' indicates their ties with the spa. An obscure political satire of 1715 tells how Martin Powell started up puppet performances in opposition to the existing Bath theatre company - certainly not later than 1709 when the show was famous enough to be mentioned in *The Tatler*, a London magazine. These and other references confirm that the puppets were in fact marionettes, which since the Restoration had come to supersede glove puppets generally. Operated by strings or thin rods from above, the costumed figures apparently stood some two feet tall and were made to perform in a miniaturised version of a real theatre with deeply recessed space, backdrop, grooved stage, wings, movable scenery, flying effects and footlights, and perhaps with some accompaniment of music. This was by no means crude knockabout theatre. A puffing tribute to Powell calls him 'one of the most dexterous Managers of human Mechanism...His Wires are perfectly invisible, his

Puppets are well jointed... and as for Punch, who used heretofore to be nothing but a roaring lewd, rakish, empty Fellow... he now speaks choice Apothegms and sterling Wit'. Together with extra diversions each performance lasted over two hours.

Powell wrote all his own material and, with his assistants (some female), delivered it himself - using the customary squeaky voice for Punch. In his first few seasons he created a score of different plays, some based on traditional tales (*Dick Whittington, Friar Bacon and Friar Bungay, Dr Faustus, King Bladud of Bath*), others burlesquing the fashionable Italian opera (*Venus and Adonis, Hero and Leander, The Destruction of Troy*), and a few simply satirising contemporary life (*The City Rake, Poor Robin's Dream*). The story of Beau Nash enlisting Powell's puppets to ridicule the wearing of boots and riding dress at Bath assemblies thus sounds entirely plausible. After his success at the spa in 1709 Powell took his show to London for the winter season, then for several years alternated between Bath and the capital with additional forays to Oxford and Bristol. Where or how frequently he performed at the spa is uncertain: we hear of 'Mr Powell's great Room' in 1715, but we know that in 1723 the puppet shows used Harrison's Assembly Rooms. By 1721 Powell was being bracketed with kings Edgar and Cole (on the Guildhall façade) as out of date. But the quality still attended the performances and Powell's own son, later in partnership with another puppeteer Yeates, seems to have kept the show running into the 1730s. Puppet shows at Bath 'flourish of course', reported one witness in 1731, and they are referred to again in 1736 and subsequently by the novelist Fielding in *Tom Jones*. Later in the century the *fantoccini* (Italian marionettes) and the *ombres chinois* (shadow puppets) also toured to Bath.

Racing see **Horse-racing**.

Raffling

A form of lottery, raffling was encouraged by Bath gift shops as a means of attracting custom. In essence it was a cross between selling by subscription, a common eighteenth-century device, and a game of chance. Fanny Burney described it more cynically in her novel *Camilla* as an easy means for a retailer to get rid of some bauble which had failed to sell at its fixed price. Once a suitably seductive object had been put up for raffle, punters were persuaded to subscribe a set sum, normally half-a-crown or half-a-guinea, and then gathered at the shop (or sent along proxies) to draw lots or gamble for the prize, often by throwing dice. As early as 1700 there were raffling booths in Gravel Walks (subsequently Orange Grove) during the season, and this area together with Terrace Walk remained the centre of the activity. Raffles 'flourish of course', the Earl of Orrery told a correspondent in 1731. Another witness, Thomas Goulding, phrased it more strongly - 'the Toy-shops, China-shops, Milliner-shops, and other Shops, are ready to pull them [Bath's visitors] in Pieces for Raffles'. Fans, lockets, snuff-boxes, even (in 1765/66) a pair of embroidered shoes, were typical prizes. An air of gallantry as well as competition pervaded the occasion of a raffle, women often being presented with the prize by their male admirers. The toymen could supply rhyming mottoes to accompany gifts, and no doubt raffle winners chose appropriate messages too.

Rambling

In contrast to promenading, rambling demanded no fellow-spectators. It was undertaken for its own agreeable sake, combining outdoor exercise with easy explorations of Bath's highly picturesque, walker-friendly countryside. The great orientalist William Jones, at Bath for a month in 1777, believed he got much more out of wandering the hills and valleys than 'those who amuse themselves with walking backwards and forwards on the parades'. The sole obstacle to would-be pedestrians was the lack of well-maintained local paths, strictly a parish responsibility. In 1775 the favourite way from Kingsmead fields over to Twerton was so out of repair a subscription was raised to improve it. In 1789 the path by the Avon to Spring Gardens was in a dangerous state, and by 1797 even the Common was being denied to walkers after the tenant farmer fenced it round and put up 'No Trespassing' signs, though protesters broke down the fence anyway to reach the paths behind Marlborough Buildings and across the High Common for the walk on Sion Hill. The grounds of Prior Park were similarly banned at times to visitors after Ralph Allen's death. Still, many ramblers refused to be daunted. Emund Rack was not put off straying, as he phrased it, 'thro that Charming wilderness of sweets', Prior Park. Popular footpaths ran across the fields to Weston, to Bathampton, over Beacon Hill to Charlcombe, from the river ferries to Lyncombe or Claverton Down, and along the river itself, and where there were no paths people used the relatively quiet network of lesser roads.

Many routes offered excellent landscapes and views over Bath itself. We find the Dean of Durham telling his brother in 1745 that he had enjoyed his strolls enormously: 'Every way the views are fine, and the Town, considering what a hole it is in, is seen from many to great advantage...'. The diary of another assiduous walker records almost daily rambles in 1743 - on the slopes and plateau of Lansdown, over to Weston, along the river to Twerton and Newbridge or to Batheaston, up Beechen Cliff, around Lyncombe and Widcombe, to see the Combe Down stone mines or Claverton racecourse. Others sauntered further afield, to Charmy Down, St Catherine's, and By Brook for example, and women were as keen to hike as men (and must have had the comfortable footwear to do it). Jane Austen several times speaks of walks to beauty spots or to points of interest like the 'Cassoon', the much talked-of but never operative caisson lock on the coal canal near Combe Hay. Closer to Bath women certainly felt safe enough to walk on their own - Elizabeth Sheridan in 1786, for example, having a favourite solitary route along the Avon, and the 10-year-old Mary Anne Galton delighting to walk with her French mistress near Prior Park 'then rich in botanical treasures'. If one 'Humble Pedestrian' voiced regret in 1791 that the relentless outward growth of Bath seemed to be burying its flowery footpaths, the many green tongues that penetrated the built-up area still invited leisurely explorations on foot. And there is in fact plenty of evidence that strollers of all kinds took advantage of what a nineteenth-century writer deemed a city unrivalled in Europe 'for the variety and beauty of its suburban walks'.

Riding and Carriage Drives

'Airings' of both sorts were encouraged by the Corporation, first in 1699 by setting aside part of the Common as an exercise ride, then from 1722-23 by paying the proprietor of Claverton Down an annual rent to allow spa visitors to resort there, and finally in 1751 by arranging for the turnpike tolls paid by horsemen and coaches on short outings to be refunded. During the season the valley routes, pre-eminently the upper and lower Bristol roads, were often crowded with riders and vehicles bent on excursions and on displaying their steeds and fancy equipage. In time even the wearisome steep ascents of Claverton, Holloway and Lansdown became more practicable for pleasure trips following turnpike improvements. Altogether John Wood estimated there were some thirty different rides leading to extensive viewpoints and features of interest - the spot on Lansdown where Bath and Bristol were equally visible, say, or the Grenvile monument. In 1778 Philip Thicknesse recommended some of the lesser-known bridleways, in particular the way to Claverton via Bathwick and Bathampton, with the option of going on as far as Freshford or South Stoke. Real enthusiasts rode out every day in fine weather, as Princess Amelia did in 1752 or a more typical visitor, Elizabeth Collett, in 1792.

Equestrianism gave both sexes a reason to indulge in all the special gear of riding hats, riding coats, boots, stirrups, and whips, and to show off fine mounts and their personal riding skills. The growing interest in *manège*, i.e. the whole art of riding, was met in 1768 by the opening of a Riding School on a greenfields site at Montpelier, Lansdown, probably under the auspices of the Earl of Pembroke. Women initially displayed the greater enthusiasm for the venture and for acquiring that 'easy *je ne sais quoi*' so desirable in stylish riding - side-saddle in their case, of course. It may be that the first instructor at the Riding School, Captain Poitier, insisted more on the niceties of dressage than did his successor two years later, Richard Scrace, a stablekeeper from London. Scrace it was who added an open out-ride to the covered Riding School in 1774, and in 1777 erected an imposing royal tennis court as well, so creating something of a sports complex but nearly bankrupting himself in the process. In the end his former assistant and rough-rider, Jonathan Dash, bought him out in 1784 and successfully piloted the establishment until the end of the century. He made up for the loss of his out-ride (obliterated in 1795 during the construction of Christ Church) by utilising another in Burlington Street nearby.

In addition to teaching horsemanship, the Riding School hired out mounts for outings and excursions, but in doing so only followed the practice of a dozen or more stableyards in Bath which also specialised in hiring out horses and coaches - among them the second Riding School,

set up by Samuel Ryles in Monmouth Street in 1788. For the many visitors who travelled to Bath by public stage-coach, or who, once arrived for an extensive stay, sent their own carriages and teams back home to save expensive livery costs, hire services were essential if they were to ride and drive about Bath. Clifton Hot-wells together with the impressive Avon Gorge was probably top choice for a longer day excursion, but Dyrham, Badminton, Corsham, Bowood, Longleat, Stourhead and other country seats were also well within range. Many riders were content with Lansdown and Claverton Down, but in each case the landowners were becoming more restrictive. In 1797 a correspondent to the *Bath Herald* lamented the further enclosure of Lansdown which, with its fresh air and inspiring vistas, had over the years 'exhilarated the mind, and contributed to restore health and spirits to Thousands...'. Two years later carriage excursionists were asked to subscribe half-a-guinea, and horse-riders five shillings, for the privilege of using either down if they were not to be treated as trespassers, since the Corporation so longer subsidised airings nor indemnified landowners for the damage it was claimed coaches and horses caused. Alternatively one could exercise at the Sydney Gardens ride or at Dash's and Ryle's establishments and be appraised by the onlookers. One morning in 1805 Jane Austen watched 'Miss Chamberlayne look hot on horseback' and recalled going more than seven years earlier to 'the same Ridinghouse to see Miss Lefroy's performance'. It seems that viewing the equestrians must qualify as another Bath entertainment.

••• See also **Circus; Horse and Carriage Sales; Rambling**.

Routs

They spawned a small vocabulary of derivative terms, from the rout-chairs, rout-glasses and rout-china hired from the upholsterer and chinaman for such occasions, to the rout-cakes and rout-biscuits specially made or bought in. Once called a 'drum', a rout was 'an assemblage of people of fashion at the private house of one of them'. In practice this meant an evening card party and *conversazione* for a crowd of invited guests whom the hostess rarely knew well. Often routs were tainted by commercialism through 'the shameful custom of Vails', in other words the tipping of servants in return for packs of cards or even for entrance (sometimes done by placing a shilling under a candlestick). But this was only one reason why they were criticised so fiercely at Bath from about 1780 onwards. Stuffy rooms crammed with card tables were bad for the health, it was argued, and worse still for morals, considering all the gambling and scandalmongering that went on and the many young people who took part. On top of that, since they so often clashed with the public balls ('cruelly' reducing attendance) and the public card assemblies, they struck damagingly at the spa's most vital entertainments and threatened to overthrow the entire 'system of rational amusements' dating back to Nash's day.

Yet in spite of every exhortation routs could not be halted, no more than private concerts or private balls. (Eventually two or three private balls were being held per night and sometimes continued until 5 and 6 o'clock next morning, the Assembly Rooms musicians having been whisked away to some grand house the moment their official engagements ended at 11 p.m.). Certainly there were many less frenetic at-homes, such as the gatherings in spring 1780 when the bluestockings Hester Piozzi and Elizabeth Montagu 'were *pitted* every night at one House or another', or in the 1790s the Monday evening receptions in the Circus hosted by Dr William Falconer's wife, or Mrs Lutwyche's Tuesday evenings which often had well over a hundred guests, half of them card players, or again the card parties at James Leigh Perrot's (Jane Austen's uncle's) in the Paragon. Katherine Plymley described a reception at Mrs Falconer's. One of the two interconnecting drawing rooms upstairs was given over to cards, she wrote, the other to conversation and needlework. 'Form is excluded & the meeting is pleasant... tea & coffee of course. Cakes, wine, ozyot [orgeat], lemonade, ice &c are several times handed about & the company all retire by 10 o'clock.' On a different occasion the Plymley party started at Mrs Falconer's and then went round the corner to the Assembly Rooms in time for the country dancing, so squaring for once the perennial conflict between public and private amusements.

Science and Natural History

'Natural philosophers' (meaning scientific investigators) could be found at Bath as elsewhere, captivated by the order of nature revealed by Newton, re-enthused at intervals by fresh scientific discoveries, and well aware of the practical contribution that amateur observers could still make. Periodic courses of lectures also fanned the interest, as did the elusive chemistry of the hot springs (which the medical faculty often and contentiously analysed), and the fossiliferous Jurassic strata on which the city lay. With regard to the geology, as John Wood pointed out, there were abundant 'miracles of nature... in the soil of Bath to excite a Man's Curiosity'. Hence local quarries and stone-mines attracted specimen hunters as well as tourists of the picturesque. Some important geological collections were assembled, notably those of the apothecary Thomas Haviland in the 1750s, John Walcott in the 1770s, and, most crucially, William Smith, father of British geology, in the 1790s by whose work the chronological sequence of the rocks at last became plain. To some amateur enthusiasts fossils were simply cabinet curiosities, commodities like old coins or Dresden china to be collected and displayed. To more serious spirits like John Walcott they held a deeper significance - 'undoubted proofs of the universal deluge... described in... Genesis', he argued in his *Descriptions of Petrifactions found... near Bath* in 1779.

This religious view of science as a key that unlocked the wonders of creation was shared by others, including Edmund Rack, founder of the Bath Philosophical (i.e. Scientific) Society in 1777. Thanks to him 'petrifactions' were among the Society's interests, but members were equally keen on experiments with light and electricity, and on discussing their colleague William Herschel's astronomical findings. One memorable meeting dealt with Herschel's sighting of a new 'comet' at a magnification of over 2000 times - the discovery of the planet Uranus, as it soon turned out to be. Although other members beside Herschel owned scientific instruments, these were rarely self-built, unlike his amazingly powerful reflecting telescopes. Robert Madden had equipment of various kinds, a collection of specimens, and an extensive library on natural history; and John Bryant avidly experimented with one of the finest electrical machines of the day, costing over £100 and, as Rack remarked, capable of discharging 'ZigZag streams of Lightning 14 Inches from the End of the Conductor'.

A similar but less splendid device, installed at the optician's shop of Benjamin Smith in [Old] Bond Street, was used to administer shocks medically, and Smith had further electrical machines to hire out. Smith's shop was a veritable showcase of useful apparatus, from different sorts of *camera obscura* and pantograph to barometers and solar microscopes. Other dealers traded in fossils, shells, minerals, seaweeds, stuffed animals and birds, even in living specimens - the water-colourist Thomas Robins jun., for example, bred butterflies, moths and other insects for sale. As garden nurseries catered to horticulturalists, so did John Jelly's short-lived botanic garden reach out to naturalists by offering subscribers surplus plants. By 1800 botany had a significant following, as the first course of subscription lectures on the subject, fully Linnaean in content, clearly testified. Yet if amateurs now took to the countryside to botanise (Prior Park was one hunting ground; Wick Rocks, north of Bath, another), other aspects of natural history were comparatively neglected. Non-sporting, observational pursuits such as birdwatching, for example, still had few devotees in spite of Gilbert White's precedent over at Selborne.

••• See also **Botanic gardens; Lectures and Readings; Menageries**.

Shooting

Firearms were used not merely in hunting and to keep down vermin, but in competitive sports. Shooting matches in and around Bath may not have been as rare as the single known instance suggests. The rules of this particular competition, held at Widcombe in December 1749, required the 21 subscribers to fire at a target card from sixty yards. They subscribed 2s. each and shot for prizes of 30s., 7s.6d. and 2s.6d.

••• See also **Duelling**.

Shuttlecock

The master-of-ceremonies who briefly succeeded Nash in 1761, the elderly Frenchman Collett, was fond of shuttlecock and encouraged the visiting *beau monde* to take it up. This created resentment at the Assembly Rooms because it affected gambling profits and, according to the musician

Francis Fleming, it cost Collett his job - since 'he might have remained in... office... had he promoted the diversion of the four aces as much as he did shuttlecock'. The game was already centuries old, but Badminton house, near Bath, takes some credit for reviving it, so it may have been introduced to spa society by the Duke of Beaufort. There was ample space to play in the larger Georgian houses as well as at the Assembly Rooms.

Skating

It was periodically feasible to skate on the Avon in severe winter weather - with fatal consequences on occasion. In one sorry case three youths skating together at New Year 1789 fell through the ice and drowned. A new natural skating rink appeared overnight in January 1800 when the recently dug Kennet and Avon Canal froze over above the site of the intended Widcombe locks.

Skittles

The old game of skittles or ninepins was played around 1700 in Gravel Walks behind Abbey Church, where the alley had an attendant in charge. Either a wooden disk or a ball was aimed at the pins and knocking all nine over for a guinea was said to be a not uncommon feat. The site in the Walks, and the fairly high stakes involved, both point to gentry participation at this date, but in general skittles was classed as a tavern game until the pastime was made illegal in 1765.

Societies and Clubs

Nationally the spread of coffee-houses (and political factions) after the Restoration stimulated a vast growth in clubs, just as burgeoning corporate and financial activity created large numbers of formal institutions. In Georgian Bath they existed at many levels, a few official and public, the majority private and obscure. Virtually all the political associations, trade companies, benefit societies, charitable organisations, masonic lodges, and other serious bodies seem to have had a sociable, convivial side, and with clubs congeniality was often the main consideration. Since Bath coffee-houses, at least in high season, tended to be dominated by visitors, societies and clubs usually met and dined at inns and taverns. In 1780, for example, the *Raven* in Abbey Green proclaimed it had the best private clubroom in Bath: a friendly society already met there and soon the Bath Musical Society (or Catch Club) followed suit with its Friday evenings.

At a different level, the landlord of a lesser pub described being favoured twice a week by a meeting of chimneysweeps who played at 'put' or 'all fours' from 6 to 7 before indulging in a tripe supper. Some societies needed entirely private accommodation, a good example being the unusually early art 'academy' around 1744 which offered drawing from the nude model - a precursor of the similar society inaugurated by Thomas Beach and other local artists in 1783. Surprisingly enough, no medical society has yet surfaced in the eighteenth-century Bath records. The spa was fairly advanced, however, in forming the 'Bath & West' in 1777 - an 'improvement' society on the lines of London's Society of Arts, except rather more agricultural in its concerns - and the Bath Philosophical Society, covering the natural sciences, in 1779. The latter lapsed in 1787 but was revived in 1798. A number of sporting pastimes also depended on club and committee organisation - archery, bowling maybe, certainly cricket, and racing.

Paramount at Bath was the belief that the upper classes who happened to be residing at the spa at any given moment constituted a great club of their own called 'the company', a never precisely defined concept founded on identities of good breeding, privilege, education, free time, landed property, dress and behaviour. Proof that this was no mere abstraction is found in the stringent social rules of exclusion from the Assembly Rooms and in the occasional heated contests to select a new master-of-ceremonies when only those within the circle of gentility were permitted to vote.

••• See also **Assemblies and Assembly Rooms**; **Catch Clubs**; **Florists' Feasts**; **Poetry Contests**.

Swimming

That 'noble Exercise of Swimming in a fine running River', to cite a medical treatise of 1725, did not tempt many Georgian adult males at Bath, it seems, and the sport was totally out of reach of women. To judge from coroners' inquests and sparse news reports, the vast majority of bathers at Bathwick, Walcot, and Kingsmead meadows - the most favoured spots on the river at Bath - were boys, adolescents and young men. Swimming was sometimes taught with the aid of cork floats, but probably few became very adept. The Avon was quite dangerous because of deceptive eddies, the uneven bed, the weir, and a heavy growth of weed. It seems less the drownings, however, than the increasingly 'offensive' sight of nude swimmers that induced the framers of the Bathwick Act of 1801 to make it illegal to bathe or strip naked for that purpose at any watercourse in the parish.

Taverns see **Inns and Taverns**.

Tennis (and Fives)

The Georgian game was not of course *Lawn* Tennis, which came to Bath only in the 1880s, but the much older and more sophisticated sport of *Royal* or *Real* Tennis. During Elizabeth's reign, when Bath was equipped with at least two courts, more was supposedly spent on tennis than on improving the baths, yet by 1700 these courts had ceased to function - though a fives court, of which nothing further is known, is marked on Gilmore's map of 1694 just outside the West Gate. Some form of fives persisted as a street game all through the eighteenth century to judge from its explicit prohibition in the Bath Improvement Act of 1793. A fresh interest in organised tennis seems to have developed in the 1730s. As part of the Queen Square development John Wood built a 100-foot-long court in the lower angle formed by Barton (now Gay) Street and George Street. Called a 'Fives Court' on Wood's own map, it was consistently referred to in the ratebooks as a 'Tennis Court' and may have served both sports. Wood paid rates on the building for only three years (1736-38) before it was stated to be 'uninhabited', its early demise doubtless brought about by the change of plan which created a line of houses on Barton Street infringing on the tennis court site. In the same period Richard Jones put up another tennis court, in Widcombe, but in 1752 this too fell prey to building development.

Around 1776 a plan to erect tennis and fives courts and a keeper's house near St James's Parade (or the north end of Westgate Buildings) was countered by an alternative proposal for a court off Cottle's Lane (now Julian Road) where Bath's first Riding School had opened in 1768. In the end the latter was preferred, thanks especially to the backing of the Earl of Pembroke, who was said to have designed the ambitious Parisian-style building in association with the Riding School's owner, Richard Scrace. There is little doubt that the Earl was a shareholder in the enterprise, for he said as much a few years later when he enquired about the court's progress. It had in fact opened auspiciously in September 1777 under the direction of a French professional, Hulet. Combining

riding and tennis on a single site had its attractions, and we hear from
one visitor that he both 'took the dust in the manege' (i.e. practised in
the Riding School) and also played tennis. But the overall proprietor,
Scrace, was now in financial difficulties and around 1780 he sold the
court to Arthur Molesworth and his daughter. Hulet resigned and a
temporary replacement had to be found from the St James's Street court
in London until Eleazor Hathway was appointed. From then on the court
seemingly prospered, because over the next 19 years Hathway made a
good living. On his retirement in 1799 he was succeeded by one
J.M.Milton (alias Meyrick or Maddock), described as not a very skilled
player but a competent marker (i.e. scorer) and 'very assiduous to his
business and civil'.

The tennis court itself, which nowadays holds Bath Industrial Heritage
Centre, was an impressive structure. At the sale of the leasehold in 1802,
the building was proclaimed 'one of the completest in Europe, not only
by the improvements on all other Courts, but... [from] its adjoining the
Riding House, and the conveniences of different exercises for health
and amusement'. But despite being still 'respectably attended by the
lovers of athletic sport' as late as 1809, it was not to last. Within a few
years the nets, rackets, and playing costumes were removed, and for a
time all the jargon of 'hazard' and 'chase', 'penthouse' and 'dedans',
was forgotten. For nearly twenty years it was employed for quite other
purposes, and then unexpectedly recovered its original function as a
tennis court for one brief period, c.1830-1835, before starting on a long
history of industrial use.

Theatre

Among various initiatives stimulated by Queen Anne's visits was a small
playhouse on north Borough Walls put up by George Trim in 1705. A
few years later a second playhouse, converted from a stable, stood just
east of St James's church by the Ham Gate. The existence of two theatres,
modest though they were, seems excessive when the season was still
short and the actors depended on plays being 'bespoken' at the whim of
visitors (command performances in effect) - unless the cut-throat
competition between John Powers' company of actors and Martin
Powell's puppet shows explains it. Rivalries among the well-to-do
patronesses who encouraged performances could easily influence the
reception of a play, as at Cibber's *Love Makes a Man* in 1716 when the
Whigs applauded a performance requested by Mrs Walpole, the Prime

Minister's wife. On this occasion the afterpiece was *The Cobbler of Preston*, since some such concluding farce, burlesque or pantomime was always expected, as increasingly was music. Songs, dances and interludes interspersed many performances, while in ballad opera it was integral to the whole concept.

When Gay's tremendous hit of 1728, *The Beggar's Opera*, was brought to Bath on the heels of its London success, the Pump Room musicians must have been co-opted, for they certainly took part in the subsequent staging at Bristol. Gay coached the Bath cast himself, the chief actresses received new costumes, and the 'quality', it was said, packed the pit and boxes for an unprecedented run. Some hint of contemporary staging possibilities, including wires and trapdoors, appears in an announcement (from Bristol) that besides Gay's production the Bath company was offering *The Siege of Troy* with 'all the Flyings, Sinkings, Singing, Dancing, Incantations, and other Decorations'. Otherwise, at this early date, scenery and props often must have been rudimentary and much re-used, although the costuming benefited markedly in 1733 from a court dressmaker's donation of royal cast-offs, plus a new set of 'Roman Shapes' and a '*Falstaff's* Dress'. These accompanied the Bath troupe on their Gloucestershire tour that summer, for since the 1720s the later start of the Bath season had made 'strolling' circuits through nearby counties more practicable.

Under the actor-manager Hornby, the performers moved in 1732 from the cramped theatre on Borough Walls (demolished in 1738 for the new Hospital) to a fresh venue in the remodelled basement of Hayes' (until recently Harrison's) Assembly Rooms. With tiered benches nearly to the ceiling this could in theory accommodate over two hundred - but not necessarily in comfort, for at a play attended by the Countess of Burlington in 1734 the room was so hot and overcrowded she had to leave. Despite the Licensing Act of 1737 which, strictly interpreted, outlawed most London and all provincial theatre, the playhouse struggled on for another decade, continually hampered by its restricted size and its terms of lease through which most of the profits went to the Rooms. As the Bristol actor John Hippisley pointed out in 1747, strangers to Bath expecting to find the best English stage outside London must have been sadly disappointed. Hippisley's untimely death left his proposals for a new theatre to be developed by others - first by Simpson, current proprietor of the Rooms, who began creating a stage and auditorium underneath the large ballroom that he was also building, and second by a consortium headed by the elder John Palmer, a local chandler and brewer, which acquired a site in Orchard Street. In the meantime the actors had transferred in 1747 to the *Globe*, an inn just outside the West Gate, but in spring/summer 1750 these - or a rival company - established a temporary theatre in Kingsmead Street where they acted such pieces as *The Beggars' Opera, Hamlet*, Lillo's *London Merchant* and Rowe's *Tamerlane*, the latter given before the visiting Prince of Wales. Barely three months later Simpson's and Palmer's theatres were both ready. Their almost simultaneous launch heralded six years of mutually harmful competition, during which time Simpson's key player, the actor-manager Henry Brown, was persuaded over to the rival camp. Beau Nash too eventually came down on the side of Palmer who then achieved a deal with Simpson's son, now holding the reins, to close down his theatre completely.

Once Palmer (who had bought out his partners too) held a monopoly, the Orchard Street theatre had room to improve - in spite of the setback of losing £1000-worth of sets and costumes in a wagon fire in May 1758 as the company was en route to the Isle of Wight. Under John Arthur's domineering management (1760-8) the theatre achieved some stability, but it was the younger John Palmer who, succeeding his father as proprietor, transformed its fortunes. To secure a royal patent in 1768 was a prestigious coup which put the Bath theatre on a legal footing at last, but Palmer also reorganised the company, imported fresh talent, inspiredly made the Bath actor William Keasberry his executive manager, extended and remodelled the stage and auditorium in 1775, and finally in 1779 secured the crucial lease of the Bristol theatre that enabled productions at Bath and Bristol henceforth to be profitably dovetailed in a joint operation.

The last three decades of the century saw the company of some thirty salaried staff at the height of its reputation. While a permanent core of stalwarts gave solidity, a regular transfusion of younger stars - Siddons, Henderson, Wallis, Incledon and others - brought freshness and excitement. Children also performed, especially as dancers, and if the theatre musicians sometimes came in for criticism (perhaps too busy with other engagements ever to rehearse much), they still included outstanding players in Brookes, Ashley, Cantelo, and Alexander Herschel. As for stage sets, the scene-painter Thomas French ranked among the most ingenious in the country - pantomime and the popular new genre of gothick melodrama giving him great scope for spectacle and special effects.

The Orchard Street repertoire looks catholic enough for the period (which nevertheless ruled out ancient or foreign classics unless in heavy English disguise). Shakespeare (in Georgian adaptation) was a perennial favourite - a score of his plays being staged 1770-1800 alone, *Hamlet* almost every season and eight others in more than 20 of these 31 seasons. Moral scruples somewhat curbed productions of Restoration drama, but modern comedies of manners, sentimental pieces, ballad opera, pantomime, and in the 1790s German melodrama, were all well represented. Local playwrights such as Sophia Lee, Hannah More, and S.J.Pratt had their turn, but it was the semi-homegrown Sheridan who most delighted the audiences. Nothing really satisfied them, wrote one of Garrick's correspondents from Bath, once they had seen *The School for Scandal* and *The Duenna* (and, he might have added, *The Rivals*). Out of all those who trod the boards Bath theatregoers fell most fervently under Sarah Siddons' spell during her outstanding four seasons 1778/9-1781/2, and welcomed her back ecstatically on guest reappearances from London. As late as 1799 crowds lined the streets for a mere glimpse of her, and the fortunate audiences honoured Siddons' emotional acting with 'rivetted attention whilst on the stage, and the loudest plaudits at every exit'. It was an intimate space to act in but that very histrionic advantage also limited audience capacity. In 1765 a new theatre had formed part of the Queen's Parade Assembly Rooms plan, and in 1779 Palmer projected an ambitious successor to Orchard Street near the present-day Podium site, but neither was built. In the end Palmer sold out in 1786 to his fellow-patentees, Keasberry and W.W.Dimond. Keasberry himself retired in 1795 and it remained for Dimond to see through the theatre's splendid removal to Beaufort Square in 1805.

••• See also **Circus; Lectures and Readings; Puppet Shows**.

Waits Music

Affluent visitors were welcomed to Bath not only by rounds of bellringing but by impromptu band pieces played outside lodgings and inns by the City Waits in the confident expectation of a handsome tip - if only to send them away. They were something like carol singers, only purely instrumental, more insistent, and usually resented. Hoping for 'favours', they also serenaded visitors in the Gravel Walks and elsewhere, a practice still being sanctioned by the Mayor as late as 1763. In fact Mrs Sneyd refers to the Duchess of Kingston sitting outside on the Parades in May 1771, 'her French Horns [most likely the Waits] playing before her; a very pretty imitation of a Country Fair'. The Waits did have a municipal function in playing in the procession at the annual Mayor-making and other civic ceremonies, and for this they were put on an official footing in 1733 and henceforth received four guineas a year. This was some belated recognition after the snub Beau Nash had administered, a generation earlier, by importing his own musicians from London for the Pump Room band. By 1774, however, a growing annoyance with the Waits, and especially protests at the disturbance they caused to invalids, forced the Corporation to ban them from playing at lodgings any more, and a year later, when the prohibition was ignored, to discharge them altogether. Even then they remained unofficially in business. The band of horns and clarinets who played at pleasure gardens and other places in the later decades surely included former Waits.

Walking see Promenading; Rambling.

Wicksteed's Machine

Thanks to the Wicksteeds, seal-engraving became an eighteenth-century Bath speciality. John Wicksteed had settled there by 1732, and in 1737, leaving his wife Sarah to take customer's orders for armorial insignia (set in gold mounts) at their Orange Grove toyshop, he removed his engraving operation to Lyncombe. Here, on a prominent site near the corner of Lyncombe Vale and Ralph Allen's Drive, stood his welcoming house and workshop (though not the portico'd 'Sigillarium' that John Wood designed for him). What made it unusual was that the engraving process was water-powered and soon attracted sightseers on their outings to Lyncombe Spa, Prior Park or the Combe Down stone-mines. A caller in 1743 found a 'marshen [machine] for Cutting Stone Seals by an Inging [engine] which goes by a water mill in his Garden which is very neat & has a good Prospect from it'. Mechanisation would have speeded the process of incising coats of arms, crests and cyphers into the hard 'Brazil pebble' he then favoured. Subsequently the range of products widened to include cameos and engraved gems, introduced perhaps by Wicksteed's son James, the proprietor from 1754.

Wicksteed's Machine' (elsewhere called a 'jewelling mill') was indicated on local maps and easily visited on foot or by carriage. From 1769 a cold mineral water spring on the site began to be exploited and a year later the property was further developed into a rural pleasure garden, the Bagatelle. The work of seal-engraving meanwhile continued up to James Wicksteed's departure in late 1773. That was not quite the end of 'Wicksteed's Machine', since James's estranged daughter-in-law Mary Wicksteed set up a rival seal- and cameo-engraving business by Pulteney Bridge which also employed a mechanical device, a variant or copy of the original presumably. By then another seal-engraver in town, Anthony Vere, likewise had a powered engraving tool at his disposal.

••• See also **Pleasure Gardens**.

Window-shopping

With its handsome streets, safe smooth pavements, rows of specialist retailers, and a highly competitive trading environment, Bath was a window-shopper's paradise. Shops went out of their way to tempt. Until a bylaw of 1766 reduced them to plain signboards, many of them flaunted hanging emblematic and pictorial signs. By the 1730s bow-fronts were coming in and soon became commonplace, since they afforded better opportunities to display goods. Here luxury shops made the running. Jewellers, silversmiths, watchmakers and toymen crammed their windows with gifts and glitter. Printshop windows resembled miniature picture galleries and often drew a crowd. Milliners, haberdashers, mercers and others draped the latest modes and fabrics. Confectioners piled up mouth-watering pyramids of sweetmeats and fruits. Dealers in porcelain, shotguns, perfumery, wigs, tea and coffee, medicines, and musical instruments, all dangled their wares before the passer-by. Butchers and poulterers were festooned with meat and game, and Mrs Piozzi even recalled the sight of a fishmonger's slab in Bath Marketplace when she was at distant Prague in 1786.

In addition the shopping trail embraced the nearby provisions market, which between 1764 and 1776 had been laid out afresh in a great arc around the new Guildhall with separately numbered stalls for dairy products, meat, fish, greengrocery, and other commodities. Viscount Torrington thought it much superior to the new market at Oxford, and the writer Robert Southey claimed it surpassed anything in London and belonged among the surprising sights of Bath. People enjoyed wandering round pricing the produce. Geese a mere six shillings, cucumbers only ten pence to a shilling, John Penrose noted with heavy sarcasm in 1766, unused to such outlandish demands. 'Green Peas at Market half a guinea a pint. Asparagus half a Guinea a hundred ...', ran a characteristic diary entry of Edmund Rack in 1780. Jane Austen too kept a keen watch on market prices, but then she was as enthusiastic a window-shopper as some of her characters - from Isabella in *Northanger Abbey* who longs for a bonnet with coquelicot ribbons she spotted in Milsom Street to Admiral Croft in *Persuasion* who could never pass a certain printshop in the same street without gazing at an unconvincing boat depicted in the window there.

Raree Show

A Note on Sources

Almost any historical publication relies on comparative information, context and ideas supplied by modern authors, and this small book is no exception. Nevertheless it is very largely based on first-hand sources (printed, manuscript and visual), includes much new material, and sometimes corrects previous accounts. Contemporary local newspapers have been the single most valuable source, but directories, guidebooks, diaries, letters, eighteenth-century history and creative literature, Corporation records, maps, prints, and other materials have all yielded valuable data. Some idea of the precise documentation may be gained from the bibliography at the end of the anthology <u>Voices of Eighteenth-Century Bath</u> *featured on the next page.*

Also published by RUTON

VOICES OF EIGHTEENTH-CENTURY BATH

An Anthology of Contemporary Texts illustrating Events,
Daily Life and Attitudes at Britain's Leading Georgian Spa

Compiled by Trevor Fawcett and published by Ruton 1995

This is a new approach to the history of Bath which lets the evidence
speak for itself. The Georgian spa survives not only in its streets and
buildings but in the echoing voices of its former residents and visitors -
voices that are captured in the hundreds of revealing and often highly
entertaining extracts presented in this volume. Some of the voices are
well-known. We listen to the composer Haydn, the artist Gainsborough,
the politicians Wilkes and the elder Pitt, Lord Chesterfield and the actor
Garrick, John Wesley and Jane Austen, Wedgwood the potter and the
future George IV. But we hear too from land developers and shopkeepers,
country parsons and wagon-owners, schoolteachers and pupils, criminals
and antiquaries, physicians and bluestockings, from the poor and obscure
as well as the great. No matter how individual and discordant the voices
may sound in solo performance, the result is a balanced chorus on
eighteenth-century Bath.

The whole anthology is arranged according to eighteen topics, each with
its own brief historical introduction:- The Developing Townscape -
Transport - Industry, Trade and Retailing - Spa Facilities and Treatments
- Visitors - Lodgings - Food and Drink - Assemblies, Gambling &c. -
Theatre and Music - Excursions and Healthy Exercise - Serious Interests
- Education - Religion - Corporation, Politics and Administration -
Disorder, Crime and Punishment - Poverty - Royalty and Loyalty - Beau
Nash and his Successors.

Taken from a wide variety of printed and archival sources, the great
majority of the extracts included will be new even to those knowledgeable
about eighteenth-century Bath.

208 pages in A-5 format   ISBN 0-9526326-0-8